GET IN THE Q ANNUAL

The crippling effect of Q9 on viewers
The antidote is *Coronation Street*.

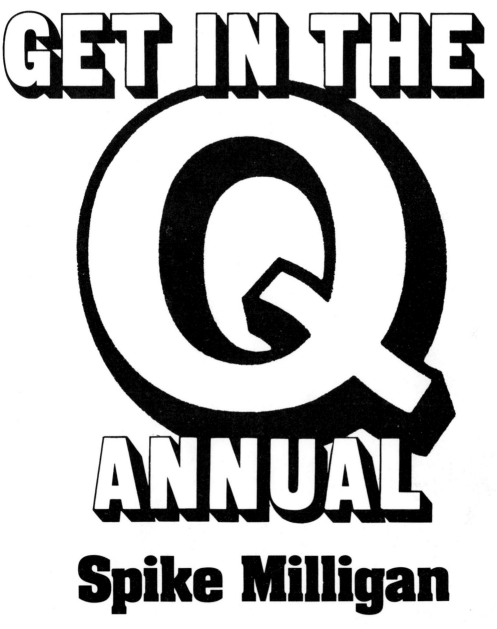

GET IN THE Q ANNUAL

Spike Milligan

Based on material written for the BBC Television
'Q' series by Spike Milligan and Neil Shand.

M & J HOBBS
in association with
MICHAEL JOSEPH
LONDON

First published in Great Britain by Michael Joseph Ltd
44 Bedford Square, London WC1B 3DU
and M & J Hobbs, 25 Bridge Street
Walton-on-Thames, Surrey

ISBN 0 7181 1962 2

Typeset in Great Britain by Granada Graphics Ltd
at Redhill, Surrey
Printed by Hollen Street Press Ltd at Slough, Bucks
and bound by Dorstel Press Ltd, at Harlow, Essex

The author and publishers gratefully
acknowledge the BBC for permission to
reproduce the illustrations on pages
9, 10, 13, 18, 26, 28, 31, 34, 37, 40,
43, 46, 50, 53, 57, 59, 60, 62, 67,
71, 74, 78, 80, 85, 86, 87, 88 and 91.

CONTENTS

MICHAEL JOSEPH LTD

Telephone: 01-323 3200 Telex no. 21322 Telegrams: Emjaybuks London WC1
Registered in England No: 304766

44 Bedford Square London WC1B 3DU
Registered Office

OFFICIAL REQUEST FOR DEDICATION

AS/LM

17 July 1980

Miss Norma Farnes,
9 Orme Court,
Bayswater,
London W2.

Dear Norma,

Here is the paste-up of GET IN THE Q ANNUAL
for Spike's consideration. Is it possible for
him to do a 'Dedication' on pages 6 and 7 (as
in the Q ANNUAL) - otherwise we have two blank
pages! Please let me know when the paste-up
is ready for collection.

All best wishes,

Yours,

Alan.

Alan Samson

OFFICIAL DEDICATION AS REQUESTED.

Oooohhh! What a fine book this is, and it hasn't even started yet. Imagine how good it will be when you are half-way in, or if you are approaching from the other end, half-way out.

Why not two of you start reading it one from each end, and arrange to meet on page 48 in a head-on collision – as you collide with the word 'and' or from the other direction 'dna'.

Thrills await you within these crisp white sheets, snatched from the hand of dysentery ward patients at critical moments.

Apart from which, any number 127 bus will take you directly to this book.

For my part I am reading *Airline Fractures*, the story of an air disaster, on which I am glad to say my landlady, Mrs Rhoda Eggs (inventor of the ugly pill), was killed outright, which apparently is the best way to be killed; anybody killed partially outright is not entitled to a death certificate.

End of dedication and application for fee.

Signed

William McGoonigal

Spike Milligan at the end of the Q Series (by permission of *The Lancet*)

THE IRISH YO-YO

Spike Irish yo-yo's, Irish yo-yo's. Get your Irish yo-yo here.

JOHN BLUTHAL ENTERS AS BIONIC RABBI.

Bluthal *(in thick Australian accent)* I'll 'ave one of them, sport.

Spike He has mistaken me for a sport – possibly squash or rowing. Why?

AT THE SAME TIME HE HANDS OVER THE YO-YO.

Bluthal *(does business with yo-yo)* It doesn't come up again.

Spike No, it's Irish. It's disposable.

Bluthal What's the difference between an Irish yo-yo and another?

Spike There's no difference – they're all the same, especially the others.

THEY LOOK AT EACH OTHER.

Spike I think we'd better stop this sketch. It's not going to lead anywhere.

Royal yo-yo sellers talking to the Queen.

Bluthal 'Ang on, 'ang on. Just a minute. You mean that's it? I've come all the way from Australia for two lines.

Spike All right, we'll let you say them again. *(to audience)* You don't mind, do you? He's come all the way from Australia. While you're saying them I'll go round with the hat ...

SPIKE TAKES HIM BY THE HAND AND LEADS HIM THROUGH THE AUDIENCE.

Spike Good luck, sir. God bless you, lady. Remember an old Jewish Australian with only two lines ... thank you, sir.

BLUTHAL CONTINUES SAYING 'I'll 'ave one of them, sport' and 'What's the difference between an Irish yo-yo and another?'

Announcer Mr Bluthal and Mr Milligan will be back again with another glittering example of how to wreck Anglo-Australian relationships. Mr Milligan is 61 and Mr Bluthal isn't.

Spike Milligan trying to remember his lines.
On the right – Bob Todd trying to forget his.

THE 5 'O' CLOCK NEWS

Spike The world record free-fall parachute was carried out today by an Irish paratrooper. He said the secret of his success was a special parachute that did not open. The Press interview took place in a hole 29 feet down.

A new organisation is offering distressed people help. They call themselves the Punk Samaritans. Should you feel suicidal, just phone them and they'll tell you how to do it.

Irishman Pat Mebot exploded today after drinking his millionth pint of stout. He is now in the record book of Guinnesses.

Sports News. This afternoon, Seamus Looney will attempt to break the eight-minute mile. Said his coach: 'If he's successful next year, he'll go for a nine-minute mile.' Looney has two coaches, both driven by his father.

An Irish Jockey created a world record today by coming in second 433 times. When asked why, he said, 'I don't know de way to the winning post, so I always have to follow the fellow in front.' Meanwhile, in the Irish Derby, fourteen horses came in a dead heat today. The board of stewards have shot thirteen so they can choose a winner.

PHONE RINGS. SPIKE ANSWERS IT.

Hallo, what, yes. Ah, there's more coming through about that story but . . . er . . . not enough. Meanwhile a Luton housewife has asked local medical authorities to switch off her husband's life support system. So they blew up the Labour Exchange.

Finally, the man who has cleaned Buckingham Palace sewers for the last 38 years was today knighted by the Queen. She used a 28-foot sword from another room.

The Body in Question

SPIKE WEARS BIG HOOTER AND AWFUL GINGER WIG AND IS DRESSED LIKE JONATHAN MILLER, WEARING SWEATER AND SHIRT, ETC.

Spike Good evening to you on the National Health Service. But if you're a *private* patient, a much better evening to you.

According to the make-up girl I am Jonathan Miller in 'The Body in Question'.

THE BACKGROUND IS A BLOW-UP OF THE FAMOUS LOURDES POSTCARD SHOWING ALL THE CRUTCHES OF THE CURED. SPIKE

IS SITTING BEHIND DESK WHICH MASKS HIM FROM THE WAIST DOWN.

Spike In 1603, Dr Jim Dalek isolated the human legs. So it's about this terrible disease that I want to talk tonight. Let's take a look at a pair – mine, for instance.

SPIKE HURLS A PAIR OF VERY RUBBERY, EXTRA LONG LEGS, OVER THE FRONT OF THE DESK, WHERE THEY DANGLE DOWNWARDS.

Spike This is the type you see hanging out of Scotsmen's kilts – but rest assured legs are *not* catching. Legs are hereditary, and run in most families. The symptoms of

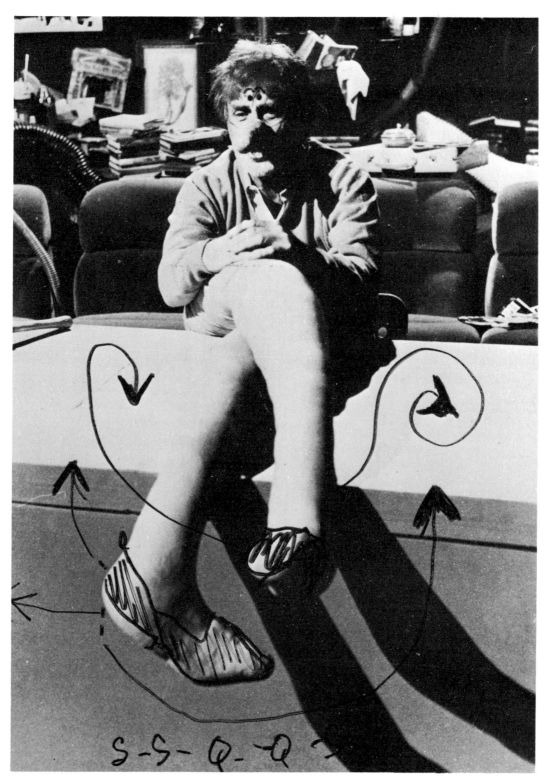

Spike Milligan trying to revive 'the Twist.

legs are this: Stand up, look down and if your bum is not touching the ground, then you've got legs. Nothing serious. Look, when you get up in the morning, give them a good counting. One, two. Or if you're face downwards, two one. Now, if they come to a total of two, that should be enough to carry you through the day. If you go out, it's sensible to cover them up with trousers – there's no need for the neighbours to know that you've got them. If, on waking, you find you've got three legs, one of them might not be. If it's shorter and the weather's been cold, it could mean your pyjama cord has frozen stiff. In cold weather this happens. A patient of mine fell out of bed and broke his nightshirt.

Now, how do we try and get our legs to work. One way is by bus. Or if you're rich, send them by taxi and they'll be waiting for you when you arrive at work. For your part, you can make your way there doing Toulouse Lautrec impressions. Remember, Toulouse Lautrec is bad enough but to lose your legs is sheer carelessness. Now, you may have an advanced condition of legs, called hairy.

SPIKE PRODUCES A PAIR OF LONG, VERY HAIRY LEGS, HALFWAY TO A GORILLA'S.

Now, if you've got legs like this and the back of your hands trail along the ground, don't see a doctor, see a zoo.

HE STANDS UP TO REVEAL A NORMAL, SINGLE HAIRY LEG WITH A BOOT ON.

Now, this is a pronounced hairy leg. H-A-I-R-Y, pronounced hairy, it means you're (A) a man, or (B) you're not. If you're a not, put on a skirt, a padded bra, stand in the Bayswater Road and see what happens. If you're run over by a bus, it means you weren't on the pavement. If you're arrested – see a solicitor. If he's wearing a skirt and a padded bra, form a limited company.

Next week I'll answer the question: can leg-irons cure a crippling overdraft? Or a major problem of our time, is sleeping alone contagious?

DESK IS WHISKED AWAY FROM SPIKE

SPIKE IS WEARING A KILT FROM WHICH HANG FOUR LEGS IN ADDITION TO HIS OWN. THESE LEGS, WHICH ARE SOCKED AND BOOTED, DRAG ALONG THE FLOOR AS HE EXITS.

Mrs Goodman

Crufts

NEW BREED DISCOVERED

INCREDIBLE SHOCK HORROR

SPIKE & JOHN BLUTHAL ENTER. JOHN IS ON A LEAD IN A DOG SKIN. HE IS SMOKING A FAG AND READING *THE FINANCIAL TIMES*. IN A TICKET BOOTH IS ALAN CLARE DRESSED AS A WOMAN. HE WEARS A BLONDE WIG, HEAVY LIPSTICK AND INFLATED BALLOON BOOBS UNDER HIS JUMPER. KEITH SMITH IS THE PERMANENT PUNTER. HE KEEPS GETTING AT TICKET, THEN CHANGES HIS HAT FROM A BASKET OF HATS AND APPROACHES CASH DESK AGAIN.

Keith Enecs dworc ymonoce cbb.

Spike No, no, no. You were reading the caption from behind.

Keith No, I wasn't. I can't read with my behind.

Spike No, I'm not suggesting you have eyes in your bum. Otherwise every time you put your trousers on you'd go blind, or – pay off number two – everytime you put your long johns on you'd think somebody was pulling the wool over your eyes; or – pay off number three – every time you sat down you'd break your glasses; or – pay off number four – every time you went to the pictures you'd have to hang over the back of the seat and pull your trousers down – but you'd have difficulty asking the lady in front to take her hat off and gawd knows how you'd eat a choc ice.

KEITH EXITS. BOB TODD ENTERS. HE IS DRESSED AS A COMMISSIONAIRE. HE WEARS A ROW OF MEDALS. HE WEARS A COMMISSIONAIRE'S HAT BUT WITHOUT A CROWN, SO THAT HIS

15

British Leyland Publicity Department.

BALD HEAD APPEARS THROUGH THE TOP. HE IS BEATING A BASS DRUM. HE IS ALSO WEARING A BLACK MASK.

Bob Roll up, roll up. Come and hear Spike Milligan try to get laughs from a dodgy audience. Roll up, roll up. Come and see genuine live doggies, as seen scoffin' grub on the TV dogfood commercials.

Spike That's 'cos they've been damn well starved for a week. Otherwise they wouldn't touch it. I mean, how do you expect a dog to open a tin of dogfood?

BLUTHAL STARTS TO PULL ON HIS LEAD AND IN THE FASHION OF W.C. FIELDS GOES 'GHRRH, WOOF, BARK, YAP, GROWL' ETC. HE PULLS AWAY.

Bob Where's he going?

Spike Usually he goes in the gutter.

Bob What I mean is, where are you taking that mangey 'erbert?

Spike Mangey 'erbert? This is a pure bred Royal Scottish Elephant Terrier.

Bob What? There aren't any elephants in Scotland.

Spike No – he finished them all off.

Bob Really? How does he kill 'em?

Spike He waits.

Bob Waits?

Spike Yes. Well, they got to die sometime.

John Woof, growl, bark, yap, grrgghh.

Spike Heel, heel.

Bob He'll what?

Spike He'll keep quiet now. No, since the elephant's gone he's had to change his diet. He's on the venison.

Bob Venison, isn't that deer?

Spike Oh, very. Eight quid a tin.

John Woof, growl, he says . . .

Spike Heel, heel. Why are you wearing that soppy mask?

Bob I thought I'd bring a touch of gypsy mystery to an otherwise boring sketch. I mean to say, I get fed up banging this thing.

Spike Well, we can all do with a good bang now and then. In any case, that mask round the minces has failed. I think you're

Convicts training to be police dogs.

trying to hide something. Here – I know you! you are the Lone Ranger: a white horse, a flash of light, a sack of spuds, some dodgy ratings and bingo, you're out of work, aren't you? Where are you hiding that poor red wog Tonto?

Bob (*beating drum*) Boom, boom, boom, boom . . .

Spike Listen. I hear the sound of a trapped tom-tom. Somebody open the window. Milligan goes bionic. (*makes noises*) Little red crosses in the eye. Moves at speed of light.

SPIKE SMASHES OPEN THE SIDE OF THE DRUM, WHICH IS OF COURSE MADE OF PAPER.

BUNDLED INSIDE IS A REALLY ABSURD SOFT DUMMY OF TONTO THE INDIAN, WITH AN IDIOT SMILE ON HIS FACE. HE HAS THE STEM OF HIS PIPE STICKING OUT OF HIS MOUTH. SPIKE BECOMES NORMAL.

Spike You see the lengths people will go to to get accommodation in London? How much are you charging him, Rachman?

Bob Only a quid.

Spike He's in a bad way. That's the only way you can get in this show. That or fly from Australia. Ah, this must be his pipe of peace. No, it isn't. It's a piece of pipe. I put that joke in for any Red Indian plumbers.

A trio of policemen in disguise catch Milligan training to be a pouf
– note fourth policeman brilliantly disguised as a drum
– and note this photograph brilliantly disguised as a joke.

Alan *(sings)* Hello, young lovers, you're under arrest . . . Here – what's that Australian actor doing in that doggie skin?

Spike Hear that, Bluthal? You got a mention. All dogs have skin, you nana. That's what holds them together. Otherwise he'd be spread all over the carpet. Bits of giblets, lung, gall bladder and wedding tackle.

Alan Pause. Gives withering stare. I still say he is not a doggie.

Spike Sing John!

JOHN SINGS.

BBC Governors observe Spike Milligan and wonder how long the poison will take

Spike That's not Bach, that's Beethoven. His bark's worse than his Beethoven.

Voiceover All right, sketch number 39, that's enough. You're becoming absurd. Come in, sketch number 39.

Omnes What are we going to do now?

John Woof.

Omnes What are we going to do now?

John Woof.

19

AMNESIA

MAN GOES INTO DOCTOR'S SURGERY.

Man Doctor, do you have anything for amnesia?

Spike For what?

Man Er, um . . . *(scratches head)*

Spike *(to camera)* For people with bad memories, here that is again.

Man Here's what again?

Spike Um . . .

THEY LOOK AT EACH OTHER CROSS EYED.

Jockeys finishing the Grand National course during a racehorse strike

THE FLYING CARPET

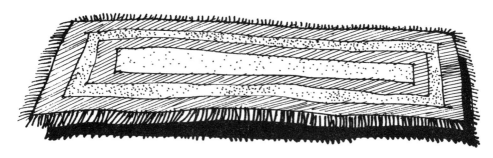

AN ORDINARY STREET. WE SEE SEVERAL CARS PARKED, BUT IN ONE SPACE THERE IS A RECTANGULAR PERSIAN CARPET ABOUT THE SIZE OF A MOTOR CAR. IN THE MIDDLE ARE TWO ORDINARY DINING ROOM CHAIRS. SEATED ON ONE OF THEM IS BOB TODD. HE IS DRESSED AS A CITY GENT. NEXT TO HIM IS HIS WIFE. SHE WEARS CLASSLESS 'GOOD' CLOTHES. BOB TODD HOLDS A MOTOR CAR'S STEERING WHEEL IN HIS HANDS.

Todd Not much room to reverse here.

Wife No. Hurry up, Garth. Here comes a policeman.

Todd It's all right, Robin – we're not doing anything wrong.

THERE IS A BACKDROP WITH CRAFFITI WRITTEN ON READING 'BBC ECONOMY LOCATION SET'. SPIKE ARRIVES AS POLICEMAN. HE CIRCUMNAVIGATES THE CARPET. HE CARRIES A BLANKET.

Todd Abracadabra *(shouts louder at the carpet)* ABRACADABRA! She's a bit cold this morning.

SPIKE TAKES BLANKET AND WRAPS IT ROUND WOMAN'S SHOULDERS.

Spike They all laughed at me at the station when I came out with a blanket, but I knew one day it would come in useful.

Todd *(shouting at carpet)* Abrabloodycadabra!

Wife Try it with a choke, dear.

(he tries to choke her)

Todd Abracadabra!

Wife Don't be such a fool, Garth.

Spike Joking aside, sir, could I see your licence?

TODD HANDS SPIKE A BANANA. SPIKE PEELS IT AND STARTS TO EAT IT.

Spike This licence is out of date. Besides, this is a combined dog and television licence.

Road testing an Axminster carpet. © Snowdon

Todd No, it isn't. You're being silly. That's a banana.

Spike Of course it's a banana. Not for one moment did it fool me. You don't think I'd eat a combined television and dog licence, do you? In any case, I didn't ask you to show me your banana. I asked to see your driving licence.

Todd But officer, you don't need a licence to drive a carpet.

Spike Let me be the judge of that, sir. Now then, I want you to blow up this bag, sir.

Todd Certainly.

TODD CONNECTS A THIN WIRE TO THE BAG. THE WIRE COMES FROM A DYNAMITE PLUNGER, WHICH TODD THEN PUSHES DOWN. THE BAG EXPLODES. SPIKE BLOWS WHISTLE.

Spike Stop, thief. I'm sorry, sir, I'll have to arrest you.

Todd What's the charge?

Spike Well, as I'm bent, it's 50p an hour, plus two quid for knackering the plastic bag. You do know, I suppose, that you are trying to drive a carpet?

Todd Tut, tut. You see, this is a flying carpet.

Spike Snigger, snigger, disbelieving snigger. All right, have you a pilot's licence?

Todd Yes.

HANDS OVER FIVE SINGLE POUND NOTES.

Spike This licence appears to be in order, sir.

POCKETS THE NOTES.

I think I've had enough of this sketch, sir. And I think the readers have had enough. Now, are you going to come quietly or do I have to use ear plugs?

CARPET TAKES OFF AND EXITS SKYWARDS

Tom

THE 6 'O' CLOCK NEWS

Spike London. Last night, rock singer Elton John filled the Albert Hall. He'd left the dressing-room tap running.

The Police have arrested Lord Frinsby Scott Scramson on the Blinns. You'll remember last year he was Court Chamberlain. Unfortunately, last week he was caught shoplifting.

Good news for British tree lovers. English Elm disease has broken out in Holland.

Vatican News. The Pope has promised Bruce Forsyth an audience. He's sending eight bus loads of nuns to the Palladium.

Sir Geoffrey Howe – and why – announced today that within six months Britain would be booming, that income tax would be down to 10 per cent and that there would be jobs for everyone. Sir Geoffrey also believes the world is flat.

Owing to a fall in standards, the Royal Navy are to reintroduce flogging. The practice will commence on Monday when they will try and flog the *Ark Royal*, two minesweepers and a mothballed stoker.

The Guardsman and The Squatters

SPIKE AS A GUARDSMAN. HE STANDS OUTSIDE A SENTRY BOX AND DOES A FEW SLOPE ARMS JUST TO SHOW HE WAS IN THE ARMY IN 1943. A PAINTED BACKDROP OF BUCKINGHAM PALACE. WE SEE SPIKE DOING ODD POSES WITH AN IDIOT GRIN ON HIS FACE – THEY RANGE FROM CHARGING ON THE RUN TO TAKING OFF HIS BUSBY AND PUTTING A KNOTTED HANKIE ON HIS HEAD. HE LOWERS HIS TROUSERS. WE PULL BACK TO REVEAL JAPANESE TOURISTS – MALE AND FEMALE. THE WOMAN WEARS A KIMONO. THEY ARE FRANTICALLY TAKING PHOTOGRAPHS.

Spike Right, that'll be 50p.

MAN HANDS OVER MONEY.

Jap Ah so.

Spike Ah so to you. I'm a merry grenadier guards sentry and I'm keeping you-know-who and Philip from all harm.

THE JAPANESE LEAVE.

Those two nice nips, they thought I was Prince Philip – of course, everybody knows I'm not. He charges a quid. I mean there is a resemblance between me and him. I mean, he's got the same number of legs and things that I have.

DAVE LODGE ENTERS. HE IS A SERGEANT IN THE GUARDS. HE IS SMOTHERED FROM HIS NECK TO THE BOTTOM OF HIS COAT IN MEDALS.

Lodge Attention, right turn. Stand at ease. Form fours. Form threes. Now then, what are your duties, Guardsman Grollix?

Spike Pardon?

Lodge Grollix.

Spike I am not Guardsman Grollix, I'm Guardsman Tom.

Lodge Just testing your memory.

Spike Stop this sketch a second. Aren't you Dave Lodge of Cockleshell Hero fame?

Lodge Funny you should say that.

Spike I don't think it was funny. It didn't get a laugh.

Lodge Which bit of the film did you like?

Spike The bit where you get mangled by the propellors of a German E boat.

Lodge I didn't get mangled.

Spike You mean you look like this

Dave Lodge showing a Guardsman the number of medals he got
for his performance in Cockleshell Heroes.

normally? What I'm trying to say is, can I have your autograph? It's not for me, it's for her. You know my husband and I don't get on, you know.

Lodge Oh really?

HE TAKES AN AUTOGRAPH BOOK OUT OF HIS OWN POCKET AND GOES TO WRITE, BUT STOPS.

Lodge Right. *(goes to write again and stalls)*

SPIKE SPELLS IT FOR HIM.

Spike D.

Lodge Yes.

Spike A.

Dave Yes.

Spike V.

Lodge Yes. E.

Spike Good. Now I know why you're a sergeant.

LODGE TAKES OUT THE PAGE AND GIVES IT TO SPIKE.

Lodge That'll be 50p.

HANDS OVER EXPRESS CARD.

Spike American Express.

Lodge Oh, that'll do nicely. Thank you.

FLOOR MANAGER (KEITH SMITH) ENTERS. HE IS VERY GAY.

Keith Hold it, hold it.

Spike He *is* holding it. You don't think it stops up there on its own, do you?

Keith *(sniffs)* Ooooh, who's got on Butch Boy? Oh, it's you, you naughty sergeant. *(smacking Dave's wrist)*
  (to Spike) You smell nice, too. What have you got on?

Spike Clean socks. With just a hint of the Imperial Leather.

SUDDENLY WE HEAR NOISE CACKLING IN KEITH'S HEADPHONES.

Keith All right, all right. Stop shouting. Or I'll never go dancing with you again. All right, they're going to start from where they left off.

Spike I wish he'd leave off. Mind you, given the chance he'd leave everything off.

KEITH EXITS, LEADING DAVE LODGE BY THE HAND.

Spike There's promotion for you.

SUDDENLY HE STOPS AND LOOKS AT THE CAMERA.

I wonder what the folks back home are doing?

CUT TO GROTTY FRONT ROOM. TERRIBLE TILE FIREPLACE. SEATED ARE AN AGED GRANDMOTHER AND A MIDDLE-AGED MAN AND WOMAN. THE MUSIC BEING PLAYED SOFTLY IN

THE BACKGROUND IS 'THERE'S NO PLACE LIKE HOME'. THEY IMMEDIATELY GO INTO A THREE-HANDED BALANCING ACT ONE ON TOP OF THE OTHER. SPIKE COMES TO THE DOOR.

Spike Oh, I was just thinking about you.

CUT BACK TO SPIKE AS GUARDSMAN.

Spike Oh they've gone and so have I. So that's what I'm doing here. Just fancy, all those years I thought they were geriatrics, and all the time they were doing balancing tricks. Meantime, Greenwich Meantime of course, back to the sketch.

SPIKE MARCHES BACK TO THE SENTRY BOX. IT NOW HAS A FRONT DOOR ON IT, COMPLETE WITH A LETTERBOX AND KNOCKER.

Spike What's going on 'ere?

SPIKE KNOCKS ON DOOR. BOB TODD OPENS THE DOOR OF THE SENTRY-BOX FROM WITHIN. HE COMES OUT WEARING LONG GROTTY UNDERWEAR AND TATTY CARPET SLIPPERS. HE WEARS A PEACE BAND ROUND HIS FOREHEAD. THE FLIES OF HIS LONG UNDERWEAR ARE HELD

Guardsman: Halt who goes there?
Bob Todd: We all do.

TOGETHER BY FOUR OR FIVE
CLOTHES PEGS, AS ARE THE
BUTTONS AT THE TOP OF HIS
VEST. HE SMOKES A HUGE
HAVANA CIGAR. HE NIPS IT OUT
LIKE A WOODBINE AND PUTS IT
BEHIND HIS EAR. HE WEARS A
LONG BLONDE WIG. HE PUTS
MILK BOTTLES DOWN. HE HOLDS
A FLORAL PO.

Spike Halt. Who goes there?

Todd We all do.

Spike 'Ere, wait, what are you doin' in
there?

Todd I'm not doing it in there. I'm doing
it out 'ere.

Spike Well, when you're in there what
are you doing out here?

Todd I'm squatting.

Spike No you're not, you're standing up.
(to camera) That, or he's a funny shape. Are
you male or female?

Todd Well, all the evidence points to
male.

Spike 'Ear that? The dirty devil's been
pointing at it. Now, you get out or I'll get
Philip to set the corgis on you.

Todd Oh, has Philip got the corgis?

Spike Yes. Very bad. All up his legs.
Picked 'em up from a dirty saddle.

Todd Polo?

Spike No thanks, I've just had a jelly
baby.

A HANGMAN'S NOOSE IS
LOWERED INTO SHOT ALONGSIDE
SPIKE, AND STOPS LEVEL WITH
HIS HEAD.

I see she's brought back hanging, then.

TODD STARTS TO SLIP THE NOOSE
OVER SPIKE'S HEAD. KEITH
ENTERS.

Keith Finished?

Todd Yes.

Keith Next set-up please.

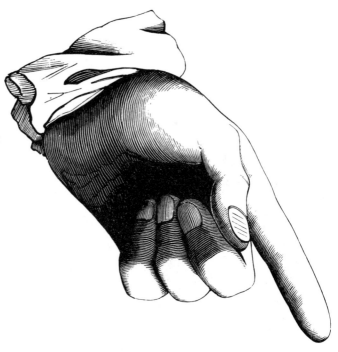

The GORILLA WIFE

A DOCTOR'S SURGERY – THE CONSULTING ROOM. BOB TODD AS DOCTOR. HE WEARS A WHITE COAT. ON THE CONSULTING COUCH THERE IS A SKELETON. BOB IS SITTING BY HER, DIAGNOSING HER ILLNESS. HE'S TAKING NOTES.

Bob Now you say you haven't eaten anything for a month?

THE INTERCOM ON HIS DESK EXPLODES.

BOB LEANS TOWARDS THE WRECKAGE, IGNORING THE EXPLOSION. Yes, nurse? *(through the intercom we hear the sound of idiot gabbling. Bob picks up phone)* Excuse me, it's my little daughter. She's just being put to bed. *(into phone)* Hallo, darling. What? You want daddy to do the sound of a doggy?

WHEREUPON HE GOES THROUGH A TERRIFIC BARKING ROUTINE, HEAD BACK, HOWLING AT THE MOON. SPIKE ENTERS. HE WEARS A SHABBY RAINCOAT AND STEEL HELMET AND CARRIES A LIVE CHICKEN UNDER HIS ARM.

Bob Bow wow. *(embarrassed laugh)* Oh hallo. Just talking to my daughter.

Spike What is she? A cocker spaniel?

Bob Now don't be silly. My daughter a cocker spaniel? She's a Jack Russell terrier.

Spike That didn't get much of a laugh – try a different dog.

Bob All right. My daughter's not a cocker spaniel. She's a Japanese shitsui.

Spike No, the shitsui never got a laugh. *(whispers)* Try something bigger.

Bob All right. My daughter's an African elephant.

Spike It's not gonna go. *(To audience)*

None of you like any of those jokes, do you?

SPIKE GOES AND PICKS A WOMAN IN FRONT ROW.

Spike Are you a woman with a sense of humour? What animal makes you laugh? Would worms make you laugh? I don't mean you'd laugh at them if you had them. I mean if there was a knock on the door and there was a worm there and it said, 'Parcel for you,' would you laugh? Here's a couple of cards. Just hold up the Yes or the No. I think she's Irish. Now would you laugh if a worm came to your door and said, 'Parcel for you'? *(reacts according to whatever she does)* How did you get in here. Through the drains? It's no good, Bob. All the jokes about the dogs and the elephants, forget all about it.

SPIKE WALKS BACK INTO SET. BOB IS NOW ON THE PHONE CLUCKING LIKE A CHICKEN. JULIA BRECK IS NOW LYING ON THE COUCH.

Puzzle Corner – which one gets it?

Spike Ah, good morning, Doctor.

Bob Oh, I'm a doctor, am I? Good. Take a chair.

Spike *(picking up chair)* Ta. I'll come for the cupboard and the tables later.

Bob Now what appears to be the trouble?

Spike This audience – I'll try a song. *(goes into an appalling 'Three Coins in the Fountain')* *(sings)* Three birds up a mountain. *(ad libs the rest)* See? Fit as a fiddle. With no airs on the G string.

Bob So you say there's nothing wrong with you at all. *(pause)* It's my considered medical opinion that there's nothing wrong with you at all. That'll be five guineas.

SPIKE PUTS HAND INSIDE HIS COAT AND LETS OUT A STRANGLED SCREAM.

Bob What is it?

Spike My wallet.

Bob This means immediate open wallet surgery.

THE DOOR BURSTS OPEN AND A GORILLA WEARING A FROCK AND A HEADSCARF TIED UNDER THE CHIN WALKS IN. IT SPEAKS WITH A WOMAN'S VOICE. SHE CARRIES A SHOPPING BAG.

Bob My God!

Spike No, no. That's not God. That's my wife Rosita.

Bob You married a gorilla?

Spike No, no. We're only living together. We say we're married because we don't want the neighbours talking.

Bob So you're living in sin?

Spike No, Deptford.

Bob Even so, living with a gorilla . . .

Spike Actually she's not a gorilla. She just wears a gorilla skin. She's got an inferiority complex. She wears it to draw attention to herself. And of course she always gets first in the queue at Tesco's. Even the girl on the till scarpered. We haven't paid a shopping bill since she started wearing it.

Bob You're wasting my time. There's nothing wrong with you that death wouldn't cure.

Spike Yes. That is why I need a very good bad serious illness. *(looks at diary)* Except the last two weeks in August.

Bob Why?

Spike Holidays. Majorca. Haven't you read it. Fourteen days of sunlit promiscuity on the back of a lorry. Thirty pounds all found — or you can find it yourself for nothing.

Bob You don't take her on holidays dressed as a gorilla?

Spike Oh no. She goes as a spotted hyena.

Bob Where does she stay?

The president of the Tommy Handley Memorial Club tells Spike Milligan he is not as funny as ITMA

Spike The zoo.

Bob Look, I want to know why you want a serious illness.

Spike I'll tell ya. I've been sticking stamps on my National Health card for thirty-eight years. Grand total, two thousand eight hundred quid. And all that time I've never had a day's illness.

Bob So?

Spike So, no illness – I want my money back or—

Bob Or what?

Spike Or I want an illness equivalent in value to my stamps – like bubonic plague, leprosy. The big stuff.

Bob *(takes out quill pen and starts to write on the paper)* Scratch, scratch, scratch, scratch, pretend writing. *(he hands paper to Spike, who reads it)*

Spike Scratch, scratch, scratch, pretend writing. I've never heard of an illness called that.

A dwarf's head massage parlour in Soho.

34

Bob Oh no, that's in code. What it says is . . .

BOB REACHES DOWN BEHIND DESK AND HOLDS UP AN IDIOT BOARD WHICH SAYS, 'REMOVE ALL CLOTHING, WAIT FOR SNOWSTORM, SLEEP NAKED BY OPEN GRAVE IN HIGHGATE CEMETERY.'

Spike Oh? Then what?

BOB TURNS THE BOARD ROUND.

Bob Now read on.

Spike Double pinu pinu pinumonia. Is that bad?

Bob It is the way you pronounced it.

Spike Will it kill me?

Bob Only once.

IMMEDIATELY SPIKE TAKES OFF HIS HAT AND PUTS ON A POLICEMAN'S HELMET.

Spike Right, Dr Crippen, the game's over.

Bob Who won?

Spike England 13, Scotland 0 – after extra time. It's my duty to tell you you are under house arrest.

Bob This isn't a house. It's a block of flats.

Spike All right then, you're under a block of flats arrest. Now I must warn you that anything you say won't get a laugh because I wrote the script and I've given all the funnies to myself. We'll start with this. Have you heard how the Irish Knock Knock joke goes?

Bob No.

Spike All right then. You start.

Bob *(very loud)* Knock knock.

Spike Who's there?

BOB LOOKS PUZZLED.

Spike You see?

BBC make up department's idea of
Spike Milligan as Larry Grayson.

BLONDIN in BRIXTON

BOB TODD AS A WORKING-CLASS MAN AND DOREMY VERNON AS A WORKING-CLASS HOUSEWIFE – FLORAL OVERALLS ETC. IN FRONT ROOM, VERY GROTTY, OF TERRACED HOUSE. THERE IS A FISH TANK ON THE MANTELPIECE WITH A HUGE FISH THAT FILLS THE ENTIRE TANK. BOB IS DRESSED AS A FISHERMAN – HE WEARS LONG WADERS, SOU'WESTER AND WHITE TIE AND TAILS. HE WIELDS A FLY-FISHING ROD WITH A GIANT HOOK. LOTS OF CASTING BUSINESS. DOREMY IS STANDING BY THE GAS STOVE WITH A FRYING PAN. ALAN CLARE IS THE GRANDFATHER OF THE FAMILY. HE ALSO WEARS EVENING DRESS TROUSERS, BUT WITH AWFUL BRACES AND THICK BELT, EVENING DRESS SHIRT WITHOUT ANY COLLAR AND A KNOTTED CHOKER – LIKE A PEARLY KING. HE ALSO WEARS A FLAT CAP AND AN AWFUL BEARD ON ELASTIC WHICH FITS UNDER THE CHIN. A LARGE SAFETY-PIN IS THROUGH HIS NOSE.

Alan Ha ha ha. I will start this sketch by saying how happy I am to be a punk rocker. I will say some rude punk rocker words – dirty socks, rubber knockers, snotty handkerchief and boils. There!

TODD CASTS THE LINE INTO THE FISH TANK.

Alan Right hand down . . . as you are.

Bob Don't worry, I'll have him soon.

Doremy Well hurry up. I've had the chips on for the last four hours.

THE DOOR BURSTS OPEN AND SPIKE ENTERS. SPIKE IS WEARING WHITE TIGHTS AND A SPANGLED LEOTARD. HE WEARS TIGHTROPE WALKER'S SLIPPERS. HE HAS A HUGE CURLING CLIP-ON BLACK MOUSTACHE AND HAS VERY, VERY BLACK EYEBROWS. HE HAS AN ASSISTANT WHO CARRIES A LENGTH OF ROPE AND A HUGE MALLET AND IS DRESSED IDENTICALLY, EXCEPT THAT HE WEARS A JACKET AND COLLAR AND TIE OVER THE LEOTARD AND TIGHTS. HE ALSO WEARS A CRASH HELMET. SPIKE CARRIES AN UMBRELLA. IT LOOKS AS THOUGH IT'S AN INTACT UMBRELLA, BUT WHEN IT'S OPENED IT HAS ONLY THE RIBS AND A FEW SHREDS OF MATERIAL. SPIKE HAS BRIGHT ROSY CHEEKS. HE IS PRECEDED BY JOHN BLUTHAL DRESSED AS PAGANINI, WITH A LEONINE WHITE WIG. HE CARRIES A CONDUCTOR'S BATON.

Spike Milligan explaining to Mrs Thatcher why the American raid on Iran was aborted.

HE RUSHES INTO THE ROOM AND CONDUCTS A MASSIVE ORCHESTRAL CHORD IN C. HE THEN RUSHES OUT OF THE SET AT GREAT SPEED IN ANY DIRECTION. ON THE CHORD SPIKE ENTERS.

Bob Ah, you've come to read the gas meter.

Spike No – I'm not going to read the gas meter. I'm waiting till they make the film.

Bob Did you hear that, Molly – they're going to make a film of our gas meter.

Doremy Oh – who's got the lead. ·

Spike The lead. I saw it on your dog outside. And I think a lead is better on the outside of a dog – I mean it's no good putting it on the inside and pulling it through.

Bob Sssshhhh – he's gonna bite. *(swings line back out of shot. It has a huge meat hook which he lowers very slowly into the tank)* Got him now. No, no. *(lifts hook out of tank)* God, that fish is clever.

Spike Clever? *(leans into tank)* Excuse me, fish, what is the sex of the Prime Minister of England. See? He doesn't know. Whatever made you think he was clever?

Doremy Just a minute – 'oo are you? No, I can do better than that. *(makes a huge gesture _ intense dramatic overacting)* 'Ooooo are you?

Spike See that. The *Evening Standard* Drama Awards are coming up – I might as well have a go for it myself. I am Blondin. *(sings and does tap dance)*

Bob Blondin? He's dead.

Spike So that's why I don't get any letters any more.

Bob Just a minute. I don't think you are Blondin. I think you are a disguised cat burglar.

Spike Why?

Bob There's a van outside with a sack of 28 cats in it, and they've all been drugged.

Spike No. They're catnapping. You see, I use them for measuring.

Bob Measuring?

Spike I get the moggy by the tail, go into a room and swing him around. If there's room to swing one, I put the rent up.

Doremy I think that's very cruel, putting the rent up a cat.

Spike Oh, we don't charge cats any rent. I mean where is a pussy cat gonna get thirteen quid a week.

Bob American Express?

Spike Oh, that'll do nicely, thank you. Now then, if ever a man needed a line it's you.

Keith Ladies and gentlemen.

Spike All right, they know who they are.

Keith People who know who they are, Robert Stigwood, in conjunction with Lew

Grade and Brent Cross Borough Council, presents Les Blondin crossing the Niagara Falls on a rope.

Spike While Keith Smith, of whom it has been said but we have no proof, is laying out the rope, I will try and cheer you up with some Benny Hill funny words. Right. *(he flips over a card. It has the word 'knickers' on it)* Knickers. *(flips another over. It has the word 'knockers' on it)* Knockers. And . . . *(turns card over slowly. It has 'balloons' on it with bra)* An outsize lady's bra. *(pops the balloons)* There, what a let down, eh? *(walks back into set. The rope is now laid out across the floor. But Bob Todd, Doremy and Alan Clare are now all blacked up)* Hallo – you been on holiday, then?

Bob No – we had a heavy fall of soot from the fireplace. Thus saving us two expensive weeks in promiscuous Majorca.

Spike Yes, folks. Sit near a sooty fireplace for your holidays.

ROLL ON DRUMS.

And now to conquer the Niagara Falls. *(puts up the umbrella)*

Bob What's that for?

Spike Balancing.

Bob I thought they were for keeping the rain off.

Spike It is.

Bob But it's not raining.

Spike That' right. That's why it's got no cloth. It's a non-rain umbrella.

Amazing picture of Blondin crossing Niagara Falls with the rope unsecured at this end, and also fishing illegally!

Blondin crossing the Falls of Niagara.

Bob This fool of a man thinks he's crossing the Niagara Falls when all the while he's in the front parlour of 33 Leech Terrace, Lewisham.

IMMEDIATELY THE REAR WALL TURNS TO NIAGARA FALLS IN FULL SPATE. SPIKE BLOWS A WHISTLE. JOHN BLUTHAL ENTERS AS A MOUNTIE WITH A SKIRTED HOBBY HORSE ROUND HIS BODY. IT IS NELSON EDDY. HE ENTERS MIMING TO A NELSON EDDY RECORD OF 'GIVE ME SOME MEN WHO ARE STOUT-HEARTED MEN'. HE'S FOLLOWED BY AN UNBENDING STREAM OF MOUNTIES – THIRTY TO FORTY. PICTURE CHANGES TO CROWD OF RED INDIANS ON HORSEBACK CHARGING TOWARDS THEM. ALL SCREAM AND FLEE EXCEPT ALAN CLARE.

Alan I am the end of this sketch, ladies and gentlemen. *(laughs)*

The Grand National as envisaged by the RSPCA.

Queen Mary, who never lived to see Q6, 7, 8 or 9 © Snowdon

ROCKET FUNERALS

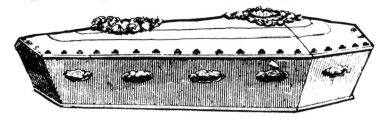

A FUNERAL PARLOUR. THERE ARE SEVERAL COFFINS AROUND. THEY HAVE NAMEPLATES ON THEM. THE COFFINS ARE CALLED 'THE BLENHEIM' 'HMS ARK ROYAL', 'CONCORDE', 'GEORGE DAVIS IS INNOCENT, OK' AND 'GOVERNMENT HEALTH WARNING: DYING CAN BE INJURIOUS TO YOUR HEALTH'. SPIKE IS SHOUTING OFFSTAGE.

Spike Get out of it, you little swines.

NOISE OF DUSTBINS BEING CLATTERED.

And a Merry Christmas to you too.

SPIKE ENTERS WITH SNOW ON HIS SHOULDERS, WEARING A MAX MILLER SUIT AND A REVOLVING BOW TIE.

Little swines, come in here asking for Christmas boxes.

SPIKE STARTS DUSTING COFFINS AND SINGING AND WHISTLING.

Fancy that, Christmas Eve and me still working. Well, it was either this or panto at Wimbledon with Noelle Gordon. I suppose she must be the first Noelle. *(terrible laugh)* I'll just open this tin of canned laughter. *(terrible raspberry)* It's gone off.

WE SEE RAYMOND BAXTER SITTING READING THE *SUN*. ALONGSIDE HIM ON A TABLE IS A MODEL OF AN APOLLO ROCKET. ON THE TOP IS A SMALL COFFIN, WITH A MODEL STIFF IN IT. THE LETTERS 'R.I.P.' ARE ON THE SIDE OF THE ROCKET. HE IS DRINKING A CUP OF TEA. IN COMES JULIA BRECK. SHE WEARS BLACK CORSETS, BLACK STOCKINGS, SUSPENDERS AND HIGH-HEELED SHOES. SHE HAS A WIDOW'S HAT AND VEIL HIDING HER FACE.

Spike Ah, good morning. *(lifts veil)* Ah, it's a lady. Good morning, Madame. *(he is transfixed)* You, er, have never played the piano accordion, have you?

Spike Milligan helping one of the audience to be sick.

Julia No.

Spike I was gonna say . . . um, what was I gonna say?

Julia Sob, sob, stifle, muffle, sob, cry, cry, cry.

Spike Have you had a bereavement lately?

Julia Yes, I've lost my husband.

Spike Well, you won't find 'im in here. They're all empty. Business is bad, it always falls off at Christmas times.

Julia Does it? Have you seen a doctor?

Spike Yes, I saw one about eight months ago. He walked past the window.

Julia They're very nice

Spike They are very nice – it's a shame we have to put them underground. They're wasted on stiffs really.

Julia Well, I don't know which to choose. You see, I'm not a rich woman.

Spike I would say you were remarkably well endowed.

Julia What's the difference between the Imperial and the Ark Royal?

Spike Well, the Ark Royal is an aircraft carrier.

Julia I don't want him buried in an aircraft carrier.

Spike Have him catapulted off the deck.

EGG-TIMER GOES OFF WITH THE

NOISE OF AN ALARM CLOCK.

Julia Oh, what does that mean?

Spike Oh, that means your time is up in the sketch. (*stage whispers in her ear*) Dressing Room 29, the whips are in the wardrobe. Sorry to have kept you waiting, Raymond . . . but well, you're a man of the world — where else?

SPIKE KNOCKS ON COFFIN LID.

Come on out, Bob.

BOB TODD CLIMBS OUT. HE HAS GHASTLY WHITE MAKE-UP AND WEARS A WHITE SHROUD MADE OF CHEESECLOTH, AND WHITE PLIMSOLLS. HE'S EATING A TERRIBLE SANDWICH AND PUTTING THE TOP BACK ON A THERMOS FLASK.

Baxter Good evening. Welcome to 'Tomorrow's World' which, owing to an industrial dispute, has been put forward to today, otherwise we would have been appearing yesterday. Which would of course automatically make today tomorrow. So welcome to 'Yesterday's Tomorrow's World'. And I'd like to thank Spike Milligan for helping bring my career to an end. (*picks up a piece of paper*) Defeat the cemetery shortage and fire your loved one into outer space. Oh? (*puts paper down*) Which brings us to this extraordinary rocket. Mr Miller, you are the owner of this establishment?

Spike Oh, am I? That's good.

Spike Milligan's dressing room.

Baxter You are the first man to deal in rocket funerals.

Spike Am I?

Baxter Yes. Can you tell me who the gentleman is standing next to you wearing the shroud?

Spike Well, a lot of people think he comes from Turin.

Baxter Why?

Spike Because he comes from Turin.

Baxter And what is his role?

Spike Oh, it's cheese and tomato.

Baxter I mean what's his job?

Spike He's a mark one trial corpse.

Baxter Would you like to describe the technical details of your rocket funerals?

Spike No.

Bob I'll explain, as I haven't had a line so far. I only took the part because of the cheese and tomato roll.

Spike *(blows whistle)* That's enough. I'm the star. You say it, Bax.

Baxter All right. This is the mark one interplanetary hearse.

Spike And the bloke what snuffs it is put in there. *(points to nose cone of rocket)*

Baxter What would you consider the most important factor involved?

Spike It's very important that the bloke in the coffin has got to be dead.

Baxter I don't believe this line. Why has he got to be dead?

Spike Otherwise the lift-off would kill him.

Baxter *(points to Bob Todd)* What part does he play, if you'll pardon the expression, in this undertaking?

Spike Until he died he was the editor of a magazine.

Baxter Which magazine?

Spike Yes.

Baxter What?

Spike Yes, he's from *Which* magazine.

Baxter But he doesn't look like a witch. He looks more like a corpse.

Spike I know. But there aren't any magazines for corpses. What corpse is gonna read a magazine – even if it was printed in a dead language.

Baxter Mr Milligan is 61 - and so is that joke.

SPIKE REACTS WITH AWFUL LOOK.

Baxter So while the poor fellow is still with us, let us go over to Funeral Control at Highgate Cemetery.

CUT TO HIGHGATE CEMETERY. CENTRE IS A COFFIN STANDING ON THE END OF WHAT IS A PIECE OF CIRCULAR LINO. AND THE COFFIN HAS STABLE DOORS – WE SEE BENCH SEAT IN LOWER HALF. ALONGSIDE IS RAYMOND BAXTER WEARING CAPE KENNEDY WHITE OVERALLS AND HARD HAT WITH INITIALS 'RIP' ON FRONT. ON HIS POCKET HE WEARS A LARGE AMERICAN EXPRESS-TYPE CARD. HE HOLDS A MICROPHONE.

BOB TODD IS STILL IN A SHROUD, WEARING WORLD WAR ONE STEEL HELMET, AND CHILD'S PADDLE POOL LIFEBELT WITH DUCK HEAD. SPIKE, STILL DRESSED AS MAX MILLER, WEARS A MOTOR-CYCLE HELMET WITH A PLASTIC VISOR WHICH KEEPS SLIPPING DOWN OVER HIS FACE. TODD HOLDS TEDDY BEAR UNDER HIS ARM.

DAVE LODGE IS HAMMERING IN ROCKETS ON EACH SIDE OF THE COFFIN, PLUS ONE OR TWO CATHERINE WHEELS AND AN ASSORTMENT OF FIREWORKS – ROMAN CANDLES, FIRE-CRACKERS, ETC. ON EACH SIDE OF THE SCREEN IS A BOY SCOUT – DRESSED LIKE IDIOT SCOUTS.

JOHNNY VIVYAN IS ONE SCOUT AND KEITH SMITH IS THE OTHER. TO THE RIGHT IS A SANDBAGGED BLAST WALL, BEHIND WHICH THE VICAR IS CHANTING THE DEATH PRAYER.

Baxter Here at the Highgate Cemetery coffin launch-pad – and I must say, it's a damn sight better than my pad – Here, it is a hive of inactivity. Mr Miller, what time is the lift-off?

Spike The lift goes off at four in the afternoon and then we have to use the stairs.

Baxter I notice the trial corpse is carrying a teddy bear.

Spike Yes, that's funny, so did I.

Baxter What's behind all this?

Spike It's a zip pocket, with a tomato and cheese roll inside.

Lodge (*with a box of matches*) The countdown is about to start. Thank the Lord for a line.

BOB TURNS TOWARDS TOMBSTONES.

Bob Stand clear, everybody. Stand clear.

Spike It's no good shouting at that lot. They're all dead.

Bob You learn something new every day.

Spike Come on.

Bob Why?

Spike 'Cos you're the corpsenaut.

Bob What's that mean?

Spike It means one giant step for man – and instant death for you.

Bob Are you mad?

Spike Yes. You don't think I would take this part if I was sane?

Baxter Excuse me, am I still in this sketch?

Spike Just! Read this. *(hands book to Baxter)*

Baxter My name is Fred Fernackapan. *(starts to sit in the coffin as he reads)* I walk about the town.
Sometimes with my trousers up,
(surprisedly) Oh! and sometimes with them down.

And when they were up, they were up,
And when they were down, they were down. *(looks at Spike)*
And when they were only half-way up.
I was arrested.
(reading) Close the door, *(does so)* and then shout, 'Goodbye, everybody'.

Spike Sing, Raymond. *(to camera)* Raymond Baxter is 72.

SPIKE LIGHTS FIREWORKS. THEY EXIT. COFFIN EXPLODES. SHEPHERD COMES ON WITH SHEPHERD'S CROOK, WEARING POLICEMAN'S HELMET. HERDS THEM OFF.

Spike Milligan before and after Q9.

the LOST PROPERTY JUDGE

11

12

8

COME UP ON SIGN, 'LEFT LUGGAGE COUNTER' AND THEN, 'THIS WAY TO JOKE'. THEN WE PAN ACROSS TO SIGN, 'RIGHT: LUGGAGE COUNTER'. BOB TODD APPROACHES COUNTER. HE IS DRESSED AS A CITY GENT, ENORMOUS PADDED STOMACH WITH THE STRINGS HANGING DOWN. HE IS WITHOUT TROUSERS. BOB RINGS BELL ON COUNTER, WHICH ONLY MAKES SOUND OF A MORSE BUZZER. IMMEDIATELY HE PICKS UP HEADPHONES AND STARTS TO TAP OUT MESSAGE. HE SENDS OUT 'MAY DAY, MAY DAY, MAY DAY'. THE MESSAGE APPEARS AS BOB TODD TAPS IT OUT. MESSAGE: 'CAN ANYBODY IN THIS SKETCH UNDERSTAND MORSE?'

WE HEAR TERRIFIC SOUND OF APPROACHING FOOTSTEPS RUNNING AT A GREAT SPEED. SPIKE RUNS IN. HE IS DRESSED AS THE LORD CHIEF JUSTICE OF ENLAND. HE WEARS HEADPHONES AS WELL. USING HIS NOSE AS A BUZZER HE SENDS A MESSAGE WHICH APPEARS ON THE BOTTOM OF THE SCREEN: 'THE LORD IS MY SHEPHERD BUT WE LOST THE SHEEPDOG TRIALS'. WHEN SPIKE STOPS, THE RUNNING FEET NOISE CONTINUES AND FADES INTO THE DISTANCE. BOB AND SPIKE TURN AND WATCH IT DISAPPEAR.

Spike When sound effects go wrong at the BBC they really go wrong. I mean, if I followed that I wouldn't be in the sketch.

Bob (*takes off earphones and puts on bowler hat,*

49

which he now raises. It has a fringe wig attached to the rim) Is this the British Railway lost property department?

Spike Yes, but we don't accept male strippers.

Bob Look, I've lost an item of clothing.

Spike Oh, I am sorry. *(puts hand on shoulder)* I lost an uncle in the Navy.

Bob Just a moment, my Lord. You did say this was a lost property office, didn't you? Normally the attendant of a lost property office is not dressed like the Lord Chief Justice of England.

Spike I sentence you to be hung. Do you have anything to say?

Bob Well, according to the rehearsal script . . .*(starts to laugh)* Rehearsal . . .

Spike Heel, heel . . .

Bob Well, I'm supposed to say, 'There's no po in the room.' *(takes off glasses)* Spike, how can you write lines like that?

Spike That line, Robert, is an integral part of the plot. Is there anybody here with a po? Don't be frightened, I've been trapped in the middle row myself. You see? There *is* no po in the room. Will you

Bob Todd reading Spike Milligan's arm.

please now say the line? We'll give you some background music. Cue organ. JOHN BLUTHAL IN STOKOWSKI MINSTREL MAKE-UP WITH WHITE WIG APPEARS ALONGSIDE SPIKE FROM BENEATH THE COUNTER. HE MOVES UP AND DOWN IN TIME WITH THE MUSIC. HE WEARS VERY OLD EVENING DRESS AND IS SMOTHERED IN DUST AND COBWEBS. MUSIC IS TOCCATA AND FUGUE IN D BY BACH.

Bob There's no po in the room.

Spike Well, don't blame me. I'm not a karzi attendant – you find judges in chambers, not in pos. And for not laughing at that gag I sentence you to Bob Monkhouse and his grin.

Bob *(gets into rage)* I don't understand what a Lord Chief Justice is doing in a lost property office without a po.

Spike Look, sir. I cannot keep up this illusion of being a judge. I am not the Lord Chief Justice, I am just a humble lost property clerk. You see, sir, people lose a lot of clobber on trains, Absent-minded judges, blokes of that ilk. *(indicates rack which has nothing but red judges' robes and a po)* What happened was the heating went off today – it all got very parky – I was so cold – you could have struck matches on 'em. So I puts on this robe and I feel lovely and warm, and I think I'll sentence you to another eight months on the Central Line.

Bob I've come to tell you I've lost an item of clothing on the train.

SPIKE IMMEDIATELY GETS A BIT OF PAPER AND STARTS WRITING.

Spike What was it?

Bob The 8.20 from Portsmouth.

Spike That's where my uncle died.

Bob He died on the 8.20 from Portsmouth? Was it the fish? Wait a minute, I thought you said he was in the Navy when he died.

SPIKE STARTS TO LAUGH LIKE MAD.

Spike Not in the Navy, in the gravy. He was in the gravy when he died. He was in the buffet on the 9.27.

Bob You said it was the 8.20.

Spike But with inflation – 9.27. Anyway, he ordered a plate of British Rail gravy and the train pulled up with a jerk. The jerk got out, and Uncle was hurled face downwards into the gravy and snuffed it.

Bob Snuffed it?

Spike You're not supposed to snuff it. You're supposed to drink it. Anyhow, he was face downwards in it and he can't swim. *That's* why he wasn't in the Navy. He tried to join and the bloke said, 'Can you swim?' and Uncle said, 'Why – haven't you got any ships?' *(laughs like mad)* For not laughing I sentence you to four years in Strangeways.

Bob But I don't have any Strangeways.

Spike Wait till you've been in there for a while.

SPIKE LEANS OVER THE COUNTER AND SEES TODD'S NAKED LEGS FOR THE FIRST TIME.

Spike I know – you've lost your trousers.
Bob No, but you're getting warm.

Spike Yeah, I know. It's this robe, it's fur-lined.

HE TAKES IT OFF AND UNDERNEATH SPIKE REVEALS AN INCREDIBLE CRAZY 'T' SHIRT WITH FEATHERS DOWN THE ARMS. IT IS VERY BRIGHTLY COLOURED AND IS SO MADE THAT IT LOOKS AS THOUGH A MASK OF EDWARD HEATH IS LOOKING OUT OF A HOLE CUT IN HIS VEST.

Bob What bizarre underwear!

Spike Well, I bought it at the church

Dave Lodge collapses after being given a line in the show

bazaar. You won't believe this, but the Pope used to wear it.

Bob I don't believe it.

Spike I told you you wouldn't believe it. Now admit it, you're here because you lost your trousers.

Bob Look, I haven't lost my trousers. I never wear them. They go against my principles.

Spike Rubs the skin off, does it?

WE HEAR NOISE OF FACTORY HOOTER.

Bob What's that?

Spike It's the hooter for the end of the sketch. You stay to give 'em a song, Dave.

SPIKE AND BOB EXIT, TAKING CLOTHES OFF AND TALKING. ON MUSIC CUE DAVE LODGE STARTS TO SING 'LAURA' AND IS IMMEDIATELY CUT OFF.

GEE UP!

Spike Milligan's version of the classic Ben Hur chariot race in modern dress.

THE 9 'O' CLOCK NEWS

Spike Good evening. There will be a historic occasion at Christie's today. Nelson's glass eye comes up for sale. Apparently it is looking for a buyer.

A priceless Ming Dynasty vase came under the hammer yesterday and was smashed to pieces.

Two Irishmen broke into Barclays Bank using Access Cards. They escaped with an overdraft of £38,000. In an anonymous phone call they have promised to pay it back over a period of six years. The police say they will not charge them with anything, but the bank said they will charge them 9 per cent interest. The anonymous caller gave his name as Pat O'Brien.

A man doing 138 miles an hour on the M1 was finally stopped by police after a desperate chase. They congratulated him because he was on foot.

A cure has been found for habitual criminals – it's called prison. One criminal said, 'It's marvellous how it works – I haven't committed a crime since I've been in here.'

The mystery concerning an Irishman, Joe Burn, who has not been seen since he set out to swin the Channel four months ago was cleared up today – apparently he's swimming it lenghwise.

A BBC Audience Researcher asks a deaf Rumanian if he likes the Q Series

55

ROYAL WINDSOR
Health Centre

AMERICAN EXPRESS ACCESS AND VISA CARDS GREEN SHIELD STAMPS

LUNCHEON VOUCHERS ARTICLES OF CLOTHING AND FURNITURE

LOSE WEIGHT and MONEY

ALL WELCOME

BACKDROP SHOWS WINDSOR CASTLE IN THE DISTANCE. IT SHOWS LINES OF WASHING ON THE BATTLEMENTS. WE HEAR THE MUSIC OF 'GREENSLEEVES'. JOHN BLUTHAL ENTERS AS HUGE WHELDON.

John Good evening, and stop that ridiculous music.

MUSIC STOPS.

I am what the make-up department fondly believes to be Huw Wheldon OBE, and pan stick. I am standing outside Windsor Castle waiting for a peerage or an idea for my new book. I am not quite sure of either title, but the book will be in the neighbourhood of £28 – and I'm glad I don't live in that neighbourhood.

Voiceover And so the great Huge Wheldon turns in his own lifetime and perambulates pontifically towards that monumental pile where he is granted admission.

BACKDROP RISES. AS IT DOES SO IT REVEALS A GROTTY KITCHEN TABLE WITH NEWSPAPERS ON IT. A BOTTLE OF MILK, TEAPOT, LOAF OF BREAD AND BROWN SAUCE. THE QUEEN (JEANETTE CHARLES) IS SEATED ON A THRON ALONGSIDE A CASH REGISTER. STANDING NEXT TO HER COUNTING MONEY IS ADOLF HITLER (SPIKE).

John *(to Spike)* Excuse me, Your Majesty.

Spike No – that's her playing zer Jewish piano.

SPIKE WINKS AT CAMERA AND STARES. IDIOT GRIN.

John Will you explain this new venture?

Spike Inflation – so Philip and his cousin, the Greek ferry boat captain Spiral Staircase, advised 'er madge to open Vindsor Castle as ein health farm. Zen her overweight subjects could lose surplus fat

Spike Milligan – a dramatic pose, i.e. unemployed.

in a patriotic gesture for the Queen.

IN THE BACKGROUND THERE ARE
THREE FAT WOMEN DOING
LAUNDRY WITH OLD—
FASHIONED WASHING BOARDS
IN ZINC TUBS. DAVE LODGE,
DRESSED AS A STORM
TROOPER, KEEPS CRACKING A
WHIP BEHIND THEM.

Dave *(continually)* Schnell, schnell – idiot
board, please – Schnell, schnell.

IN THE OPPOSITE CORNER A FAT
MAN IS CLEANING PRINCE
PHILIP'S POLO BOOTS, ANOTHER
FAT MAN WITH A JEWELLER'S
EYEPIECE IS REMOVING REAL
JEWELS FROM THE CROWN AND
REPLACING THEM WITH PASTE,
ANOTHER IS POLISHING A
SADDLE. ANOTHER IS POLISHING
A POLO STICK. THEY TOO ARE
WATCHED BY A STORM TROOPER
(KEITH SMITH) WHO CRACKS THE
WHIP AND CALLS OUT
'SCHNELLER, SCHNELLER'. A BIG
FAT LADY COMES IN.

Spike Just a minute – a customer.

SPIKE GRABS THE WOMAN'S
HANDBAG AND EMPTIES IT IN
FRONT OF THE QUEEN.
IMMEDIATELY HE GETS THE
MONEY TOGETHER. THE QUEEN
GATHERS UP THE LOOSE
CHANGE.

Spike See that. Zis big fat slob has only

been here a minute and she's lost thirty pounds already. Say thank you, Your Majesty.

TERRIFIED SUBJECT CURTSIES.

Woman Thank you, Your Majesty.

Spike Now step on this speaking weight machine. Schnell, schnell.

WOMAN GETS ON WEIGHING MACHINE. TERRIBLE SQUEAKING OF SPRINGS. AGONISED AMPLIFIED VOICE FROM INSIDE MACHINE.

Voice Ooooohhh, corrrrghh, get 'er off.

Spike See, the treatment's working – she's getting off already. The German joke – followed by ze Englisher silence. Ha, ha, ha . . . I'll come again . . .

HE STARTS HITTING THE WOMAN WITH A KAPOK STICK.

Spike Now to get a few more pounds off.

WOMAN SCREAMS IN AGONY.

John Is that expensive?

Spike No – just painful.

John I don't understand these slimming treatments. For instance, why are they washing Prince Philip's underwear?

Spike Well, it's a good drying day.

John Are they overweight?

Spike No, they're over here. Canned laughter, please. Now, what's your trouble?

John I've got acute appendicitis.

Spike Here zat? He's got appendicitis and he thinks it's cute.

AS SPIKE AND JOHN ARE TALKING SPIKE RELIEVES HIM OF HIS WRIST-WATCH, HIS WALLET AND FOUNTAIN PENS, AND GOES THROUGH POCKETS REMOVING ALL LOOSE CHANGE, WHICH HE GIVES TO THE QUEEN. SHE PUTS IT IN THE TILL.

John Where does all this money go?

Spike Haven't you heard of the Duke of Edinburgh wig appeal?

John You mean the Prince is balding?

Spike It's coming out in handfuls. Especially when he comes in late – she is grabbing him by zer barnet, shouting, 'Ver have you been now – not ze Bunny Club again . . .?'

John And there you have it. A bald futur staring him in the head or will the Tories become Whigs again? So therefore let us have another look at that knockdown of Muhammed Ali by Gladys Cooper.

RUN FILM OF HENRY COOPER KNOCKING DOWN CASSIUS CLAY TO THE TUNE OF 'GREENSLEEVES

A seaman swinging the lead to find the depth of Wembley football pitch.

Ireland's Olympic entry for the three-legged race.
The man behind is a fake.

An Attack of the Aarggh-Jim-Lads

CORNER OF A POSH RESTAURANT. THERE ARE FOUR TABLES, EACH WITH DUMMY ARAB SHIEK SITTING OPPOSITE LIVE, HUGE-BOOBED YOUNG GIRLS. BOB TODD ENTERS. HE IS DRESSED IN RAGS. HE IS ACCOMPANIED BY JULIA BRECK, WHO IS STUNNINGLY DRESSED.

Bob Waiter.

SPIKE ENTERS. HE IS DRESSED AS ROMAN CATHOLIC PRIEST WITH HOLY WATER CONTAINER AND SPRINKLER. HE SPRINKLES THEM WITH WATER.

Spike *(in plainsong)* Verily, I hear you call.

Bob Waiter, I'm Lord Hughmay De Nightoulon. I booked a table for two.

Spike You'll have to stand.

Bob Why?

Spike You didn't book any chairs.

Bob I'm not gonna stand for that.

Spike *(sings)* You don't have to stand for chairs, you sit on them.

Bob What's the chef's speciality?

Spike Ladies' underwear.

Bob What do you fancy, Mrs Grollix?

Julia The doorman.

Spike Sorry, ma'am, the doorman's off. But we have a nice lift-boy. Any particular wine, sir?

Bob Yes.

Spike Yes what?

Bob Yes, any particular wine.

Spike Would you like a vintage?

Bob No, just a bottle.

Spike I'll tell you what you'd like. My sister.

Bob Is she on the menu?

Spike No, she's on the bed upstairs.

Bob What year is she?

Spike A very good year, sir. Twenty-one.

Bob I thought '67 was a very good year.

Spike In that case you want my mother-in-law.

Bob Is she on the menu?

Spike No, she's on the pill. *(sudden eruption from Spike)* Arggh Jim lad, arggh Jim lad.

AS HE ERUPTS, A VERY GROTTY GREEN 'TREASURE ISLAND' TYPE PARROT APPEARS ON THE END OF A LONG POLE, WHICH IS RESTED ON SPIKE'S SHOULDER.

Spike Sorry, sir, I've been getting these attacks of arggh-Jim-lad ever since I had lunch with Bernard Kilometres.

Bob You mean Miles.

Spike No, he's been metricated. *(parrot appears)* Arggh Jim lad. Arggh Jim lad.

CAST ALL STOP AND LOOK AT EACH OTHER.

Bob Look, Spike, where's this sketch leading?

Spike Finchley Labour Exchange.

Spike Milligan helping Dave Lodge on his way to obscurity.

FINCHLEY
Labour Exchange

NO COLOUREDS —
EXCEPT RED, BLUE
AND GREEN.

Only unemployed people
need not apply

APPOINTMENTS STRICTLY BY
APPOINTMENT ONLY

AMERICAN EXPRESS
WILL DO NICELY. THANK YOU

Q9 CAST STILL UNEMPLOYED

GRATEFUL NATION GIVES THANKS

Mrs Thatcher suggests
etraining and deportation

LORD GRADE INTERCEDES
"FORGIVE & FORGET"
HE TELLS BILLY COTTON

DOWN TOOLS
(A Doctor Looks Back)

NHS DOCTORS DOWN TOOLS

Shop steward Lord Hallmit tells BMA: WE WANT THR NICKER A WEEK MORE IN READIES SHOCK HORROR

CUT TO A DOCTOR'S SURGERY. ON AN OPERATING TABLE LIES DAVE LODGE WITH WHITE MAKE-UP AND PING-PONG BALL EYES. A CHARLADY (DOREMY VERNON) IS DUSTING THE ROOM AND DUSTS HIM AS WELL. SHE PUTS FEATHER DUSTER UNDER THE SHEET AND DUSTS HIM OVER – OR UNDER.

Doremy 'Ere isn't this Dave Lodge, the Cockleshell Hero?

VARIOUS PARAPHERNALIA OF A DOCTOR'S SURGERY – INCLUDING A LARGE CASH REGISTER, AN OLD-FASHIONED ONE WHERE A BELL RINGS. THE DOCTOR IS PLAYED BY BOB TODD IN A WHITE JACKET. HE HAS A THROAT-VIEWING MIRROR ROUND HIS HEAD, A STETHOSCOPE, AND A SET OF SPANNERS IN HIS TOP POCKET. HE'S LOOKING AT A SMALL TELEVISION SET WHICH IS DISPLAYING CEEFAX. ALONGSIDE SITS HIS NURSE, JULIA BRECK. SHE IS DRESSED AS A NURSE-CUM-SECRETARY.

Bob Take this down.

NURSE PUTS PENCIL TO PAPER

Bob Chelsea 0, Albion Rovers 69. Blast.

Nurse Is that with a 'b'?

BOB STARTS TO LAUGH. LOOKS AT CAMERA.

Bob According to the rehearsal script *(pauses)* Rehearsal *(cries with laughter and pulls himself together using string, gum arabic and a postage stamp)* Any moment now, Spike Milligan should come through that door as a working-class illness.

Spike *(voice off)* Keep going, Bob – I'm having trouble with the truss.

Bob *(looks at script)* He'll be wearing a cap, grotty raincoat, 1943 trousers and carpet plimsolls.

64

SPIKE ENTERS DRESSED MAGNIFICENTLY AS NELSON.

Spike Sorry. I went to the wrong dressing-room. They're doing Lady Hamilton in the next studio.

Bob Who is?

Spike Everybody. Anyhow, pretend I've got working-class clobber on, all right? And I'm ordinary working-class.

Bob Right. Name?

Spike Lord Horatio Nelson.

Bob Don't be silly, you're supposed to be Bert Trousers, apprentice gas fitter.

Spike *(very declamatory)* Ladies and gentlemen, do I look like Bert Trousers, apprentice gas fitter?

AUDIENCE RESPOND 'NO!'

Bob *(places stethoscope against TV screen)* What's this? Brighton 3, Hove 2?

Spike That's wrong. In the Navy we say heave to.

Bob All right, then: Brighton 3, Heave 2. Well, Lord Nelson, what's your job?

Spike I'm an apprentice gas fitter.

Bob Now, Lord Nelson, apprentice gas fitter, what appears to be the trouble?

Alan Clare training for lunacy

Spike A disability of a private, marital non-bionic nature.

Bob Would you like to amplify that?

Spike Certainly. *(picks up bullhorn and repeats)* A disability of a private, marital, non-bionic nature. Oh, oh, oh, ohhhhh.

Bob I think I've got that.

Spike Oh, so you've got it as well, have you? Oh, oh, oh, ohhhhh.

Bob What?

Spike I'll do it again. Oh, oh, oh, ohhhhh.

Bob Yes, but what is it?

Spike What do you mean, what is it? I'm the patient, you're the doctor. You're supposed to diagnose the symptom of oh, oh, ohhhhh. That's why you're dressed like that.

BOB TAKES DICTIONARY.

Bob Here it is. O. Fifteenth letter of the alphabet. An exclamation or a bad football result. I'm sorry to have to tell you that you're suffering from the fifteenth letter of the alphabet or a bad football result.

JOHN BLUTHAL COMES IN DRESSED AS LIEUTENANT HARDY. HE TALKS LIKE NOEL COWARD.

John My lord, the French Fleet are drawing nigh, and are starting to bombard us. Shall we return their fire?

Spike Yes, all right. And you might as well give them back the fridge and the hallstand while you're at it.

Bob Did you hear that, nurse. These two have been at it.

Spike Run up a signal: 'England expects as much money as possible from the Common Market.'

Bob How dare you two lunatics come into a Harley Street Surgeon's consulting room *(rushes to the door. pulls door knob, which comes off)* Now get out.

Spike How? Obviously through the keyhole. *(walks over to door)* Abracadabra.

DOOR OPENS WITH HEAVY CREAKING SOUND AS IN HORROR FILM.

This door used to be in 'Aladdin'.

AS THEY OPEN THE DOOR WE SEE THAT IT LOOKS LIKE THE WOODEN DECK OF AN OLD MAN OF-WAR WITH MATCHING RAILINGS AND RIGGING DISAPPEARING UPWARDS. WE SEE THE SEA WITH CUT-OUT FRENCH GALLEONS, AS IN A FUNFAIR SHOOTING GALLERY.

Bob My God, I've got back projection.

BLACK POLYSTYRENE BALLS START TO HURTLE LIKE MAD IN ALL DIRECTIONS. THEY START TO GET BIGGER AND BIGGER. HUNDREDS OF BLACKENED PING PONG BALLS DROP FROM ABOVE,

Why Bjorn Borg always wins Wimbledon.

BOUNCING ALL OVER THE SET.

Spike All right, Dave, the sound effects.

DAVE TAKES A MICROPHONE FROM UNDER THE SHEET, WHISTLES INTO IT LIKE FALLING BOMBS, AND DOES EXPLOSIONS. THE EXPLOSION SOUND IS 'POUFF'.

Spike Yes, it's David Lodge, the Whistling Pouff. Good heavens, the show ends in forty-five seconds. We haven't a minute to waste.

BOB, JOHN, SPIKE, NURSE, START FIRING AIR RIFLES AND SHOUTING 'BANG, BANG.' ALL THE SHIPS GO FROM SIDE TO SIDE –

THEY ARE HELD BY HAND. SPIKE THEN PICKS UP A BUCKET OF WATER AND THROWS IT OVER WHOEVER'S HOLDING SHIPS OUT OF SIGHT. KEITH SMITH, WEARING UNIFORM OF A FRENCH ADMIRAL, APPEARS SOAKING WET.

Keith Stop in French. Je surrender. Vous 'ave sunk our chips and soaked my clothes Therefore vous win
the battle, a coconut and a teddy bear made from the hairs from David Attenborough's legs.

Spike And that concludes the final episode of David Attenborough's 'Life on Earth'. Terrible life, isn't it?

A funny moment in Q9   © Snowdon

NEWS AT TEN

Spike Good evening. It's been another great day for British sport. And the accent is on British because no other country was taking part. With the British were the Irish, the Welsh and, if you'll pardon the expression *(spits on floor)* the Scots. There was also a large English contingent, which we haven't managed to open yet. Who writes this stuff? No wonder David Coleman wouldn't do it. It is, of course, the annual criminal and police sports at Wormwood Scrubs. So over to Dartmoor and Eddie Waring a rather cheap BBC suit.

In the Irish bye-elections, 10 per cent voted for the candidate, 20 per cent voted against him and 70 per cent marked their papers 'Don't know'. The 'Don't know' candidate got in by an increased majority.

The tanker 'Highland Chief' went aground today with 300,000 gallons of alcohol creating a whisky slick 130 miles long. The police have been called in to hold back 48,000 Scotsmen who have volunteered to drink the beach.

At a sale of Impressionists at Sotheby's today, Mike Yarwood fetched two hundred thousand pounds. The buyer was Sir Harold Wilson.

Irish convict Paddy Moloney has taken two years to tunnel out of Strangeways Gaol – which is a pity as he was only in for a year. The Governor has given him a credit note for 21 months which can be used at any of HM Prisons.

Mr Howard Smith, the portrait painter, has been commissioned to paint Prince Philip. However, after one undercoat of white emulsion the Queen said, 'I can't go out with him looking like that.'

The
PIANO DROUGHT
A Story of The Yukon

WE HEAR A RECORDING OF RUSS CONWAY AND MRS MILLS BOTH PLAYING ONE OF THEIR TUNES AT THE SAME TIME.

MORNING STAR: 'THATCHER FORCES UNEMPLOYMENT AMONGST WORKING-CLASS PIANISTS SHOCK HORROR'

SUN: 'CRISIS IN PIANO WORLD SHOCK HORROR'

DAILY MAIL: 'LORD LONGFORD VISITS PIANO-PLAYING RAPISTS IN PRISON'

THE FINANCIAL TIMES: 'PIA... SHARES CRASH ON STOCK EXCHANGE – AND BREAK GLASS ROOF'

MELODY MAKER: 'DUDLEY MO... JUMPS TO DEATH FROM PIANO STOOL. PETER COOK GOES SOLO SHOCK HORROR'

CUT TO SHOP FRONT.

SIGN SAYS: THE HAROLD WILSON HONOURS LIST PIANO SHOWROOMS.

PROP: LADY FALKENDER, DSO, VC AND BAR.

FURTHER SIGN: GRAND PIANOS.

PAN ALONG TO: SOME NOT SO GRAND.

PAN FURTHER ALONG TO: SOME UPRIGHT AND SOME DOWNRIGHT.

INTERIOR OF PIANO SHOWROOM. ONE UPRIGHT PIANO AND ONE GRAND PIANO SURROUNDED BY SEVERAL MANGLES, EACH WITH A PIANO STOOL. HUW WHELDON STANDS CENTRE, HOLDING A BOOK UNDER HIS ARM – *ROYAL PIANOS*. NEXT TO HIM STANDS SPIKE, DRESSED IN OVERSIZE BLACK JACKET AND STRIPED TROUSERS AND HUGE SHOES. HE WEARS A LIFEBELT.

Wheldon I am standing next to Mr Dick Trailer and he is standing next to me.

CAPTION: 'HUGE WHELDON, MULTIPLE OBE'

Spike There has been a drastic reduction in the staff, and it's me.

Wheldon And it's him.

Spike I earn a modest wage – £32 per week.

Wheldon Plus a small allowance of 50p per child.

Spike This brings my money up to £280 per week. You see, Huge, my wife is a devout Roman Catholic.

Wheldon And you?

Spike I'm a practising sex maniac.

Wheldon And of course you practise on her.

Spike Yes.

Wheldon Doesn't her church advocate the rhythm method for birth control?

Spike Yes, but I got it wrong. I put on a record of 'The Woodchoppers Ball' and it got stuck.

Wheldon And what about the record?

Spike That was eleven times in one night.

Wheldon I see, then this is a part-time job?

Spike Yus. I am a Securipianist. *(points to armband with a piano and a fist holding club with spikes in it. Armband is yellow, piano and fist in black).*

BOB TODD NOW ENTERS. HE WEARS A FLORAL MID-CALF ASCOT FROCK, BLACK SOCKS HANGING DOWN, WHITE PLIMSOLLS, BALLOONS AS BOOBS. HE ALSO HAS ON A BLONDE WIG WITH RINGLETS DANGLING.

Bob *(to audience)* There's been a reduction in staff and it's him.

Spike Look, I just told them that.

Bob How did it go?

Spike Well, I'll give you an action replay.

WE SEE AN IMMEDIATE ACTION REPLAY OF SPIKE'S JOKE.

Bob Ta. *(puts bullhorn to mouth)* Get your lovely pianos here! Lovely ripe pianos!

Wheldon Just a minute. I notice that in fact most of the pianos in here are mangles.

Spike Yus. There's a simple answer to that.

Wheldon What does that mean?

Spike It means I can understand it. You see, not everybody finds the piano easy to play.

Bob *(through bullhorn)* Correct!

Spike Whereas a mangle needs no special skill at all. I'll demonstrate. *(he sits down on piano stool in front of mangle and holds piece of sheet music. He winds the mangle and sings 'Don't Cry for me Argentina'.)*

Wheldon Most original and enterprising But I didn't hear any music coming from the mangle.

Spike Well, of course you didn't. You don't get music out of a mangle. You get laundry out of that.

Wheldon They get laundry out of that, and I got a line out of it. Now I must leave – I have pressing business.

Spike Oh, going to iron your trousers, are you?

Wheldon I have an idea for a new book. shall call it 'Bloody Expensive'. *(he exits)*

Bob I'm glad he's gone. Now I'll get a few lines. Here comes one now. *(through bullhorn)* Lovely, delicious, ripe pianos. Only fifty pence a pound. Stock up on pianos now for the winter.
Keep a leg of piano in your deep freeze and have fresh piano all the year round. A free plastic jelly-mould with every pound of Bechstein.

Spike *(looking at Bob)* Why all this perve gear?

Bob I've got a kinky dresser. He won't let me wear any knickers.

Spike You mean your answer is blowing in the wind. I mean it's a good job we

Mrs Honita Wretch auditioning for Q9 – she reads from an Equity card.

haven't got a polished floor, then.

Bob *(blows whistle)* Time to start work. Now you're new here and the first thing I want to know is have you had a medical check?

Spike Yus. Three pound eighteen for a truss.

SPIKE GOES TO PIANO. HITS NOTES AND CHECKS THEM OFF ON AN ABACUS.

ENTER KEITH SMITH WEARING COMIC CUTS BURGLAR OUTFIT. HE CARRIES A BAG MARKED SWAG, A JEMMY IN ONE HAND AND A TORCH IN THE OTHER.

Keith Ha, ha, ha. Hallo, my good fellow, I'll give you a million pounds if you can guess what my job is.

Spike It's clear to me you are a forger and also a maker of counterfeit pound notes.

Keith What a lucky guess. And here is your million pounds.

Spike A million pounds. This won't go far.

Keith And why not?

Spike I only live next door. You see, I like to be on the job first thing in the morning.

Keith Yes, I heard you playing the 'Woodchoppers Ball' record. *(to audience)*

Tee, hee, hee. My disguise has fooled him, and he's the store detective. Actually I am a piano thief.

IMMEDIATELY KEITH GOES TO UNSCREW THE PIANO.

Bob *(goes to upright piano and removes the front, behind which is a gas meter)* Right, I'll just read the number of notes you've used for the last quarter. Six thousand four hundred cubic notes. You been playing concertos?

Spike No, I've only been playing pianos.

Bob Ah, but there's a standing charge.

Spike Doesn't affect me – I've been playing sitting down.

WE HEAR A CRASH AND LOOK OVER TO SEE A GRAND PIANO WITH THE EXTREME SINGLE LEG OFF AND THE PIANO RESTING ON THE GROUND. WE SEE KEITH SMITH PUTTING PIANO LEG IN SWAG BAG.

Keith Now – ha, ha, ha – for the other two.

Spike Stop, pianoleg thief. And roll VTR for the pay-off.

WE HEAR ANOTHER LOUD CRASH. PIANO IS NOW FLAT ON THE FLOOR WITH A PAIR OF LEGS – DRESSED LIKE KEITH SMITH – POINTING OUT FROM UNDERNEATH. SPIKE, BOB AND JOHN RUSH OVER.

Spike 'Ere, he's trapped by the Bechsteins. Quick, take his shoes and socks off.

Bob Why, are you a doctor?

Spike No, I'm a chiropodist.

THEY START PUTTING ON SURGEON'S GOWNS AND MASKS.

Now listen Keith, this may sound silly to you – it sound ridiculous to me – but it may sound silly to you. Are you all right under there?

Keith Yes. Perfectly all right. And for my first number I'd like to sing that lovely song that made P.J. Proby bankrupt: 'Have you seen my Willie this morning?'

"But yesterday you said you were Elizabeth Taylor."

WE HEAR INSTANTLY HARRY SECOMBE SINGING 'WE'LL KEEP A WELCOME IN THE HILLSIDE'. THEY START TO PULL THE LEGS, WHICH STRETCH LONGER AND LONGER.

Spike My God, it's not Keith Smith, it's Harry Secombe.

Bob What's he doing under the piano?

Spike Can't you hear? He's singing 'Come Home Again to Wales'.

Bob He'll never get to Wales with that piano on top of him.

THE RECORD FLUCTUATES WITH THE PULLING OF THE LEGS. BY NOW THEY'VE REACHED THE AUDIENCE WITH THE LEGS.

Yes, we'd better go and get a stretcher.

Spike Stretcher? You can't stretch him any longer than this. *(suddenly looks at watch)* It's time for 'The Woodchoppers Ball'.

SPIKE RUSHES OFF TAKING CLOTHES OFF.

Spike Milligan's father's workshop, 1931.

The Burglar's Access Card

5224 631 23456 72
1255 VALID FROM 12/79 UNTIL END 11/81
NATIONAL WESTMINSTER BANK

INTERIOR OR BANK. A BANK
CLERK'S POSITION

Clerk Hallo, I am a merry bank clerk.
I'm married with eighteen children and
one vasectomy. My pay, £60 a week. After
muggings, £12.50p. Ah, here comes a
valued customer – I'll close the position.
*(puts up sign – POSITION CLOSED – BLACK
PLAGUE*

SPIKE DRESSED AS CITY GENT
ENTERS. HE APPROACHES BANK
CLERK BUT IS PUSHED ASIDE BY
ARAB (JOHN BLUTHAL) WITH
ASSISTANT ARAB (DAVE LODGE).

Arab Out of the way, infidel scum.

Clerk Oh, good morning, sir *(to camera)*
It's his Imperial Putridness, Sheik The
Drips Off. He's come in for his daily
million pounds.

Arab Maleesh, shufti kush, have a
negayla and beguine the begin. *(and spits in
clerk's eye)*

Clerk Thank you, sir. *(wipes his eye)* I love
your sense of humour, sir.

THE BANK CLERK PUSHES A BIG
BAG OF MONEY ACROSS THE
COUNTER. THE ARABS DEPART
WITH THE MONEY. JULIA BRECK
WALKS IN. SHE WEARS A VERY
CLOSE-FITTING TOP AND A
FLOWING SKIRT.

Spike Thinks. If I had dem wogs' money
I could have her just like that. Therefore I
shall now do a robbery.

IMMEDIATELY SPIKE DIVES
UNDER JULIA'S SKIRT, JULIA
LOOKS DOWN OVER SHOULDER.

The SAS trying to free an imprisoned British bank manager.

Julia Excuse me.

Spike Yes, madame.

Julia Do I know you?

Spike No, we've never been introduced, madame.

Julia Well, what are you doing down there?

Spike Well, I know it must look bad from where you are – and it doesn't look too good from down here either.

Julia If you don't stop I shall call the manager.

Spike There's no need to do that, madame, I'm quite capable of managing on my own.

Clerk Are you being seen to, madame?

Julia I think so.

CLERK LOOKS OVER COUNTER.

Clerk What are you up to down there?

Spike I'm up to the lace on her St Michael's.

SPIKE HAS NOW TAKEN ONE OF JULIA'S STOCKINGS OFF WHICH HE HAS PULLED DOWN,

REMOVING HER SHOE IN THE PROCESS.

Spike *(to camera)* Now then, if any of the two and a half million pound train robbers are looking in – this is where you went wrong. You didn't wear a stocking mask. Watch this hold-up and learn.

HE PULLS STOCKING MASK UP OVER LEFT TROUSER-LEG.

Right. This is a robbery.

Clerk On – morning, Mr Dempster.

Spike You recognise me?

Clerk Yes.

Spike But I've got this stocking mask on.

Clerk You're supposed to pull it over your face.

Spike *(pulling stocking up leg)* It'll never reach. Look, I've no time to waste on bad jokes, read this.

SPIKE HANDS OVER A NOTE WHICH THE BANK CLERK READS.

Clerk Chislehurst Laundry Complaints Department. We regret to inform you that we are unable to accept your underwear in the condition you've sent it. We are sending it to our solicitor.

Spike That's all in code. You'll never break it, try as you may. Therefore I shall have to tell you what it says. It says, 'This is a robbery. Don't move or I'll shoot.'

Clerk That's a motor horn.

Spike Is it? No wonder I couldn't get a gun licence for it.

SPIKE TURNS THE HORN ROUND AND HOLDS IT LIKE A WEAPON.

Spike Come on – hand over the money.

Clerk Have you any means of identification, sir?

SPIKE PRODUCES A WANTED POSTER FOR JOYCE McKINNEY, 'WANTED FOR KIDNAPPING AND POLICE STAG DINNER'.

Clerk That's not you.

Spike Course it isn't. It's bad enough having to hold up a bank with an unlicensed motor horn without having to do policemen's stag parties as well.

Clerk Very well, sir – as long as you don't take too much.

SPIKE HOLDS OUT A HUGE SACK. THE CLERK HOLDS UP FIFTY PENCE AND DROPS IT IN. SPIKE CLOSES NECK OF SACK AND SWINGS IT ON TO HIS SHOULDER.

Spike *(to camera)* At last the big time – Wait a minute, what was that?

Clerk Fifty pence.

Spike Fifty pence. The taxi cost me one-eighty to get here.

BOB TODD HAS NOW TURNED UP BEHIND SPIKE, WEARING A BURGLAR'S EYE MASK AND HOLDING A PISTOL.

Bob Hurry up, mate – there's other people waiting to do robberies here.

BOB PUSHES PAST SPIKE AND HOLDS UP PISTOL IN ONE HAND AND A BURGLAR'S ACCESS CARD IN THE OTHER. CLERK LOOKS AT CREDIT CARD.

Clerk Ah yes. *(keeps putting stacks of money on the counter tied up with rubber bands while Bob Todd borrows Spike's sack to put it in)*

Spike How do you do that?

Bob Burglar's access card – takes the waiting out of wanting.

German entry for the Eurovision Song Contest with their hit song:
"Where have all the Hitlers gone?" (unplaced).

nspector McHardon's Identikit

INTERIOR OF A POLICE CHARGE ROOM. SPIKE PLAYS INSPECTOR McHARDON. HE WEARS A LOOSE OVERSIZE TRILBY, A KNACKER OF THE YARD RAINCOAT. BIG MAGNIFYING GLASS, ELASTIC GINGER BEARD UNDER THE CHIN. BOB TODD AS POLICE SERGEANT. SPIKE IS INTERVIEWING A WOMAN. ON A BLACKBOARD THE SERGEANT IS COMPOSING AN IDENTIKIT PICTURE. WE ALREADY HAVE HIS HEAD, WHICH HAS A HUGE SCARLET WIG.

Spike So the attacker had a broad forehead and scarlet hair.

THE SERGEANT PUTS BROAD FOREHEAD SECTION ON IDENTIKIT BOARD.

Woman He had narrow cheekbones.

SPIKE ECHOES EVERY WORD SHE SAYS. THE SERGEANT PUTS NARROW CHEEKBONES ON THE BOARD.

Woman And a heavy pronounced chin.

Spike Chin, pronounced C-H-I-N. Right, flash that description the entire length of this street.

IMMEDIATELY A POLICEMAN RUSHES IN WITH A MAN MADE UP EXACTLY THE SAME AS THE IDENTIKIT.

Spike Such then is the power of modern-day police detection and comedy sketch-writing.

Woman That's not him.

Spike Oooh?

Woman He was taller.

Spike Stand on those two phone books.

MAN IMMEDIATELY STANDS ON PHONE BOOKS.

Woman That's him!

Spike Fancy the tall ones, eh? I arrest you for standing on these two phone books and posing as the man who originally attacked this woman and left her unsatisfied.

Spike I must warn you that anything you say will be taken down and sold to the

Daily Mirror at the going rate of £1,000 a page. Now under the law you're allowed one phone call.

CRIMINAL DIALS A NUMBER ON THE PHONE ON THE CHARGE DESK. THE PHONE ON THE OPPOSITE SIDE OF THE DESK RINGS. SPIKE PICKS IT UP. CRIMINAL INDULGES IN HEAVY BREATHING AND SOTTO VOCE OBSCENITIES ENDING UP WITH, 'Knickers with little moth holes in certain places.'

Spike It's for you, ma'am.

SHE TAKES THE PHONE

Spike I'll trace this.

HE STARTS TO FEEL ALONG TELEPHONE LINE, WHICH IS CONNECTED DIRECTLY TO OTHER PHONE.

Criminal Listen, darling – black silk stockings filled with ice cream. And Playtex bra's stuffed with hot sponge pudding. *(hangs up)*

WOMAN STARTS TO CRY.

Woman He's hung up.

Spike Aye, we all have our hang-ups, ma'am – except for those who have them hanging down.

SPIKE HAS NOW ARRIVED AT THE PHONE BEING HELD BY THE CRIMINAL.

According to this length of GPO telephone cable you are the managing director of Obscene Phone Calls Anonymous, a secret organisation devoted to giving old ladies the kiss of life on the telephone after six o'clock when it's cheaper. For this you could go to prison for ninety years – in fact you might even get life.

Criminal What's the charge?

Spike *(produces bugle from pocket)* Well, as I remember it, it was –

SPIKE PLAYS BUGLE CHARGE. CUT TO BLACK-AND-WHITE FILM OF OLD WESTERN SHOWING US CAVALRY CHARGE.

Spike Yes, another sketch saved by the 14th US Cavalry.

The original script writers of Q9.

SEXUAL
hindrance

JOHN BLUTHAL STANDING OUTSIDE EXTERIOR OF SHOP. SIGN READS 'SEXUAL HINDRANCE SHOP. PROPRIETORS: THE POPE AND MARY WHITEHOUSE.' BLUTHAL IS DRESSED AND MADE UP TO LOOK LIKE HUW WHELDON.

Bluthal Good evening and OBE. According to my researchers I am the late Huw Wheldon. I am standing outside the world's first sexual hindrance boutique. An attempt by the late Lord Longford to suppress the ever-growing number of sex shops in the Mall.

IN THE SHOP WINDOW THERE IS A VICTORIAN MANGLE.

It's made a good start with this Victorian mangle. This small red manual, not to be confused with the Black Emmanuelle, tells how this mangle can reduce sexual permissiveness.

ON FILM

CAPTION: 'A DEPARTMENT OF SEXUAL HINDRANCE INFORMATION FILM.' CUT TO HEAD AND SHOULDERS OF RITA WEBB

Rita My husband was a sex maniac. I couldn't take any more of it, but that has all stopped since I bought my sexual hindrance mangle and dropped it on him.

STUDIO

BLUTHAL IS NOW INSIDE THE SHOP

Bluthal Yes, words of encouragement from a woman who'd had no sleep for thirty years.

WE PULL BACK TO SHOW SEVERAL MODELS OF MEN AND WOMEN. ONE WOMAN HAS A CAGE DEVICE ROUND HER BOOBS SO

THEY ARE UNTOUCHABLE AND BARBED WIRE ENCLOSING HER HIPS. ANOTHER MALE DUMMY WEARS AN ORDINARY SUIT, BUT WEARS A TERRIFYING WOODEN CRICKETER'S BOX OVER HIS GENITAL AREA. IT HAS NAILS PROTRUDING OUTWARDS. THEIR FACES ARE THE USUAL INANE SMILING DUMMIES FROM A SHOP WINDOW. ANOTHER WOMAN WEARS A BATHING COSTUME – HAS A SACK OVER HER HEAD AND PULLED TIGHT OVER HER BOOBS. AN IRON BAND WITH A PADLOCK ON IT IS BINDING HER TWO LEGS TOGETHER JUST ABOVE THE KNEE. A WOMAN IS WEARING A BRA WITH NAILS STICKING OUT AND A PAIR OF BLOOMERS, WHICH LOOK LIKE CHAIN MAIL AND ALSO HAVE NAILS PROTRUDING OUTWARDS. ANOTHER DUMMY WEARS STOCKINGS WITH HORRID VARICOSE VEINS PAINTED ON THEM.

SPIKE IS BEHIND THE COUNTER. HE WEARS A NUN'S HABIT AND SMOKES A CIGAR, WITH NO PRETENCE TOWARDS FEMALE MAKE-UP. BEHIND SPIKE IS AN ASSORTMENT OF SHELVES, AS IN A SWEET SHOP. ON THE SHELVES ARE A SELECTION OF MALLETS, ARMY BOOTS, BOXING GLOVES, SAWS AND HORROR MASKS.

Bluthal Good morning and OBE. I am Huw Wheldon.

Spike You filthy swine. I know you're here because you want it – well, you won't get it.

Bluthal Madame, I assure you that even if you had it, I wouldn't want it.

Spike I've never had it. I don't want it. In fact I don't even know what it looks like.

Bluthal Tell me, what would you recommend to help me curb my lunchtime BBC Club sexual urges?

Spike Put on this mask of Billy Cotton Jnr. (*as Bluthal puts on the mask*) You'll find he looks better from the inside. And blow up this inflatable 137 bus to Hackney.

Bluthal How can an inflatable 137 bus to Hackney stop me having sex?

Spike How? Because it gets in the way, you perverted swine you.

Bluthal Ah, here comes a client now.

KEITH SMITH MADE UP TO HAVE A WHITE BALDING WIG, WHITE STRINGY BEARD, STONE WHITE FACE WITH HUGE BAGS UNDER THE EYES. SUIT SHOULD BE OVERSIZE SO THAT IT HANGS LOOSELY ON HIM, DITTO SHIRT. HE'S ACCOMPANIED BY JULIA BRECK, WHO WEARS A MINI SKIRT, TIGHT WHITE JUMPER, AND IS MADE UP TO BE BLOOMING WITH HEALTH.

Spike Good heavens, it's Mrs Ryeckyadyk and her man.

Smith Mother, help me stop it, just during dinner time . . . *(keeps muttering and slapping back of neck)*

Bluthal Mr Ryeckyadyk, how old are you?

Smith Nineteen.

Bluthal Nineteen. Here is a case proving that the honeymoon *has* to end sometime. And when were you married?

Smith Half-past ten this morning. I've got to stop it.

Spike You sex-crazed fool, you, ravishing this poor helpless girl who's been brought up by the nuns and brought down by you. I'll just sedate him.

SPIKE BELTS HIM WITH A MALLET.

Now then, when the throbbing starts tonight, make him drink this. *(hands Julia bottle of liquid)*

Julia Before or after?

Spike Instead of.

SPIKE BELTS SMITH WITH MALLET AGAIN.

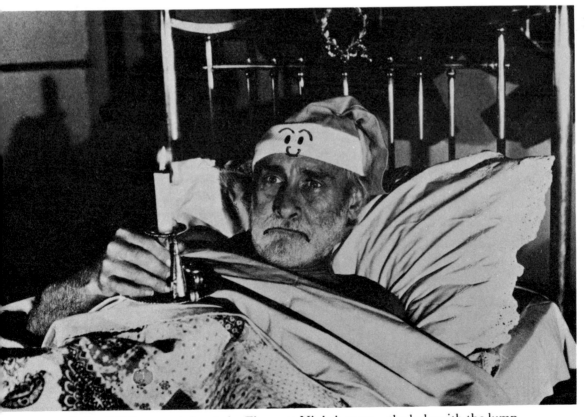

Spike Milligan training to be Florence Nightingoon – the lady with the lump.

A deputation to 10 Downing Street to stop Mrs Thatcher having more children.

Spike There, that's stopped the raging fires in his steaming St Michael's.

Smith God bless you, Mother.

THEY EXIT.

ALAN CLARE COMES IN. HE HAS STONE WHITE MAKE-UP AND HUGE BAGS UNDER EYES. HE WEARS SHIRT, BRACES, TROUSERS AND SLIPPERS. HE WALKS UP TO SPIKE.

Clare Please help me or I will go blind.

Spike It's terrible – eighteen weeks ago this man was the Archbishop of Canterbury.

Clare I was a holy man until I met Mrs

Thelma Vaseline, runner-up in the 1963 Miss Pelvic Massage Contest.

Spike Don't worry, your Grace, I'll soon have you off her and back on hymns.

Bluthal And here we see the sexual steamroller steriliser about to affect a cure on the Archbishop of Canterbury.

CUT TO FILM OF THREE OR FOUR NUNS ON A STEAMROLLER SINGING 'ALL THINGS BRIGHT AND BEAUTIFUL' BEARING DOWN ON ALAN CLARE, WHO IS STAKED OUT ON THE GROUND.

Clare Oh good, to think I'll be cured of sex soon.

THE STEAMROLLER APPEARS TO GO OVER ALAN. FROM THE BACK OF THE STEAMROLLER A FLATTENED LIFE-SIZE PHOTOGRAPH OF ALAN CLARE EMERGES.

BACK IN THE SHOP . . .

SPIKE ENTERS CARRYING THE FLATTENED PICTURE OF ALAN CLARE UNDER HIS ARM. THE PHOTO NOW IS DRESSED IN THE FULL CEREMONIAL REGALIA OF THE ARCHBISHOP OF CANTERBURY, MITRE AND ALL.

Spike Here's the dear Archbishop back to his normal self. We've ironed out his problems – and a number of other things as well. Now, I'll douse your raging BBC Executive fires of lust. *(sings)* All things bright and beautiful, All creatures great and small.

SPIKE PULLS BACK BLUTHAL'S TROUSERS AND SPRAYS AEROSOL DOWN THE FRONT OF THEM. BLUTHAL STANDS UP AND LOOKS ECSTATICALLY TO THE HEAVENS.

Bluthal It's all gone.

SCREAM FROM JULIA AS SHE RUNS INTO THE SHOP. CLOTHES NOW RIPPED AND TORN TO REVEAL THAT SHE'S WEARING STANDARD PERVE GEAR UNDERNEATH.

Julia The drink didn't work. He's been at it ever since we left the shop.

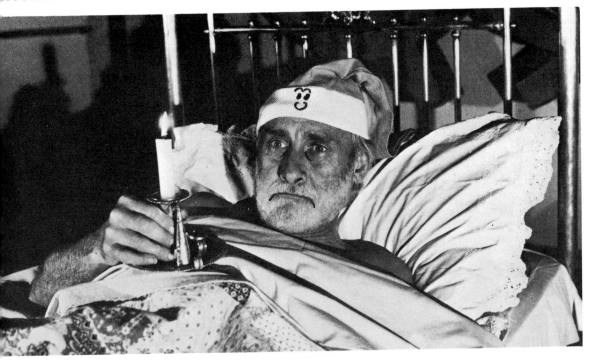

Here I am again.

THERE IS AN EXPLOSION OFF. IN THE PLACE OF HUW WHELDON ARE JUST SOME CHARRED CLOTHES, A PAIR OF BOOTS AND AN OBE.

Spike There, what a noble soul lies there ... and there ... and there. It's no good, I can't stay in this sketch any longer ... Farewell, cue applause.

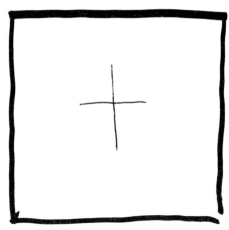

Cross Word for Idiots.

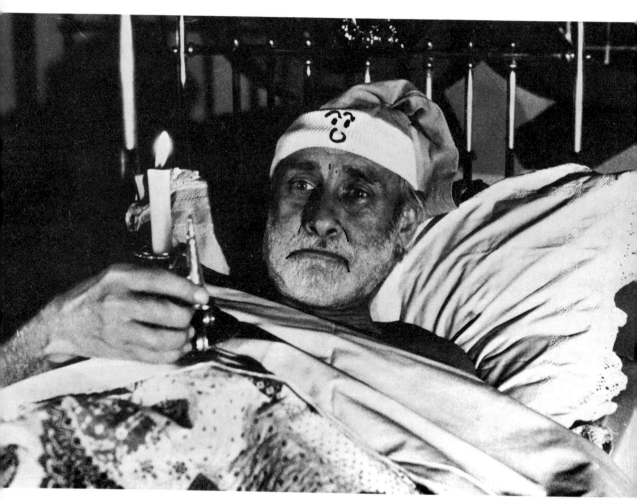

– and again.

EUROJOKES

Announcer And now, Eurojokes. National variations on the theme of Waiter, waiter, there's a fly in my soup.

A DINER IS AT A TABLE. SPIKE IS THE WAITER.

Spike England

Diner Waiter, waiter, there's a fly in my soup.

Spike Oh dear.

Katie Boyle England, three points.

Spike France.

BOTH DINER AND SPIKE CLIP ON MOUSTACHES

Diner *(very French)* Waiter, waiter, zer is a fly in my soup.

Spike Do not worry, zir, the spider on the bread roll with get eem.

Katie Boyle France, un point.

Spike Germany.

DINER AND SPIKE PUT HITLER MOUSTACHES ON. THE DINER PUTS ON A SPIKED GERMAN HELMET.

Diner *(very German)* Herr ober, herr ober, der ist ein fly in meine zuppe.

Spike *(takes out pistol and shoots it)* Jewish swein.

Katie Boyle Germany, sieben pluntz.

Spike Israel.

THIS TIME DINER AND SPIKE PUT ON BIG NOSES.

Diner *(very Jewish)* Vaiter, vaiter, der's a fly in mein zoup.

Spike Dat will be a pound extra.

Katie Boyle Israel, nebbish points.

Spike Ah shut up.

KATIE BOYLE WALKS OFF.

Spike Ireland.

SPIKE AND DINER PUT ON CURLY WIGS AND WHITE TEETH.

Diner Waiter, waiter, der's a fly in my soup.

SPIKE CLIMBS ON CHAIR, TAKES JACKET OFF AND DIVES.

Spike Don't worry, zir, I'll save him.

SPIKE DIVES INTO SOUP PLATE.

QUASIMODO

A GROTTY BUILDING WITH A
SIGN: NOTRE-DAME LABOUR
EXCHANGE, IRISHMEN EXTRA.

A LABOUR EXCHANGE DESK.
THERE IS A WALL BEHIND WITH A
DOOR. CALENDAR ON WALL,
SAYING 1963. BENEATH IS A
VOLUPTUOUS NAKED PIRELLI
CALENDAR GIRL.

TERRIFIC NOISE OF CHURCH
BELLS RINGING. BELLS STOP. A
DRAWN-OUT SCREAM AND A BODY
HITTING GROUND. FROM BEHIND
THE DOOR WE HEAR SPIKE, AS
QUASIMODO, SHOUTING.

Spike Sanctuary, sanctuary.

PAUSE.

Spike Sanctuary, sanctuary – and this
bloody door's stuck. Therefore I'll come
through the wall.

HE PUSHES THROUGH PRE-CUT
SECTION OF WALL NEXT TO
DOOR. WALKS OVER TO
CALENDAR OF NAKED WOMEN.

Spike (*reads*) It's ye olde Pirelli calendar –
what does it say? Think of me when you
tear one off.

HE PULLS A MONTH OFF.

SPIKE IS DRESSED AS
QUASIMODO. HE HAS AN
EXTRAORDINARY LARGE HUMP
ON HIS BACK. HE WEARS A
WOOLLEN SHIRT, SO NO MATTER
WHERE THE HUMP IS PLACED IT
WILL STAY IN POSITION. HE HAS
HALF A PING-PONG BALL PAINTED
LIKE AN EYE ATTACHED TO AN
ELASTIC BAND TO GO ROUND HIS
HEAD.

ALSO A LARGE PAPIER MÂCHÉ
SCHNOZZLE DURANTE NOSE,
AGAIN HELD ON BY ELASTIC. HE
WEARS WRINKLED BROWN
TIGHTS AND PLIMSOLLS. HE HAS
LOTS OF INDIVIDUAL CELLULOID
TEETH WHICH HE KEEPS
STICKING IN HIS MOUTH AND
WHICH KEEP FALLING OUT.

Spike I'm so ugly. I'm so ugly. Oh yes,
I'm ugly. Yes indeed, they don't come
uglier. Just in case some of you didn't get
that, I'm ugly. Give me a U, give me a G,
give me an L, give me a Y, it spells –

NOTHING FROM AUDIENCE, SO
SPIKE SAYS:

That's right, it spells – silence.

ALAN CLARE ENTERS WITH FACE

Keith Smith's only way of getting a laugh.

MADE UP AS WHITE AS DEATH.
SMALL TOOTHBRUSH
MOUSTACHE. HE WEARS BROWN
WORKROOM OVERALLS WITH
C&A ON THE POCKET.

Clare Ha ha ha. You don't know me.

Spike Good.

Clare Are you having trouble trying to establish a character?

Spike He looks like a compulsive blood donor!

Clare Ha ha ha. You are wrong. I am England's first bionic plumber. Have you had a leak lately?

Spike In these tights it's impossible. It's not only impossible, it's unpassable.

Clare Aren't you the Hunchback of Notre-Dame?

Spike That's my brother. I'm the Hunchback of Notre Catford.

Clare I smell a rat.

Spike There must be better things to smell than that.

WE HEAR THE SOUND OF COCONUT SHELLS BEING HAMMERED TOGETHER. ENTER BOB TODD DRESSED AS THE LONE RANGER, EXCEPT HE WEARS A BOWLER HAT. HE IS ACCOMPANIED BY JOHN BLUTHAL DRESSED AS TONTO. THEY ENTER TO THE MUSIC OF 'WILLIAM TELL' OVERTURE.

Spike (*to camera*) A blinding light, a snow white carthorse, a sack of spuds, it's the stoned ranger and blotto.

Todd Wrong, pardner. I'm the loan bank clerk.

Spike What a bit of luck – I could do with a loan. – I could do with a laugh as well.

Bluthal (*making totally out-of-sync and incorrect Indian hand-signs*) Me not blotto.

Spike You could've fooled me! Come to think of it, anybody can.

BLUTHAL GOES FORWARD WITH SMALL AXE TO KILL QUASIMODO.

Todd Hold it, Tonto.

Spike (*to camera*) Hold it? He must be wearing trousers like mine.

Bluthal Off-white man with umpty back speak with forked y-fronts. If you Quasimodo, why you not stuck up bell-tower.

Spike De rope broke. Thank heavens the ground broke my fall.

TODD GOES FOR HIS GUNS, PULLS THEM OUT, REVEALING TWO BANANAS WITH PISTOL HANDLES ON.

Todd Where I come from, that's fighting talk.

Spike (*to Tonto*) Where is he from?

Bluthal Stockton-on-Tees.

Spike Those aren't guns – I can tell a banana when I see one.

Todd OK, tell it then.

Spike (*to banana*) I can tell you when I see you.

ENTER JULIA BRECK.

Julia Oh fie.

Todd What's *she* doing in this sketch?

Spike With what she's got, she doesn't have to do *anything*. I'll get the ratings of this show up if it's the last thing I do.

Todd I can feel my ratings going up.

Clare Stop! You are not the Long Stranger. You're the man who played the log-biting canary in that last sketch.

TODD BREAKS DOWN COMPLETELY AND STARTS TO WHISTLE.

Todd He's right, I can't live a lie.

Spike Look, I've had enough of this sketch. I'm not playing opposite a retired canary. And if the audience don't like it they can read from this idiot board.

AT HIGH SPEED A LARGE BOARD IS WHEELED IN. THE WORDS ARE PRINTED ON IT A LA DANCING-HALL SONGSHEET AT THE CINEMA. SPIKE TAKES BLACK POINTER WITH WHITE PING-PONG BALL ON END.

BOARD IS WRITTEN AS FOLLOWS: THANK GOD THEY'RE FINISHED.

Tom (later)

A captive BBC audience
waiting for the show to start.

THE LATE NEWS

Spike Today veteran golfer Mr Albert Nibblick died from an excessive amount of alcohol. A Guinness lorry ran over him. Said the driver for a spokesman: 'It was very strange, he looked perfectly all right before I hit him.'

Police said the gang who stole the Grand National Winner Red Rum are looking for a fence.

A pair of Queen Victoria's knickers are coming up for sale. It'll be the first time they've been up for 79 years.

Foreign news: in Israel a sarcophagus has been discovered bearing the inscription 'First Jewish suicide'. The body had no marks, but a slip of papyrus clutched in the hand read, 'A hundred to one Goliath'.

A man was arrested in Hyde Park for feeding the squirrels. He was feeding them to his dog. The dog was last seen running up an elm tree trying to save his nuts for the winter.

Finally, the Queen is golding a harden party at Puckingham Balace. I beg your pardon, I'll read that again. The Queen is golding a harden party at Puckingham Balace.

Noodgight

SPIKE'S SHIRT FRONT FLIES OFF – IT IS PULLED FROM THE TRAPDOOR ON TOP OF ANNOUNCER'S DESK. AS HE LOOKS DOWN, WIG FLIES OFF.

And that is the end of the news. It 's also the end of the book.

Omnes What are we going to do now? What are we going to do now?

6/10